THE PURPLE HEADED MOUNTAIN

MOUNTAIN

MARTIN THORNTON

THE FAITH PRESS
7 TUFTON STREET LONDON SW1
MOREHOUSE-BARLOW CO. INC., NEW YORK

FIRST PUBLISHED IN 1962

REPRINTED 1962

© *The Faith Press Ltd., 1962*

PRINTED IN GREAT BRITAIN
in 11pt. Baskerville type
BY THE FAITH PRESS LTD
LEIGHTON BUZZARD

THE PURPLE HEADED MOUNTAIN

To My Godchildren
with love

JOHN BENEDICT HARRIS

SUZANNAH GRACE CLARK

PREFACE

BY THE

ARCHBISHOP OF CANTERBURY

THIS is a book, at once practical and profound, about the calling of a Christian. That calling is likened to the climbing of a mountain, purple-headed because the way of ascent is the way of penitence, and penitence is that right view of one's state before God which enables true vision instead of a vision clouded with unrealities.

It is, therefore, a book which points the reader uncompromisingly towards the heights : but at every point there is a down-to-earth practicality about its treatment of the spiritual life. This practicality is bound up with the doctrine that all things are created by God, and the things of every day give the context of Christian *efficiency*. The note of 'efficiency' sounds through the book; the Christian must be efficient in prayer, in meditation, in repentance, in virtue.

As you read on you are likely to feel the book to be an exciting one : exciting in its break with some of the conventions about religion which treat it as a thing apart, and exciting also in its claim that some practices which might be thought exacting are really within the reach of all. So the book moves on to some episodes in our Lord's life in their bearing upon our own. And it ends as it begins, with the purple-headed mountain where in penitence we discover that :

> 'All things wise and wonderful
> The Lord God made them all.'

MICHAEL CANTUAR :

AUTHOR'S PREFACE

THIS is not a 'Lent Book' in the sense of a carefully planned set of spiritual exercises, nor is it a systematic guide to the elements of Christian life and prayer. I attempted the latter in my *Christian Proficiency*, to which the reader can refer if he wishes to fill some of the many gaps in this rather untidy little book.

Any hope I have that it may prove useful derives from the fact that it tries to deal with some of the points and problems which constantly crop up in ordinary pastoral practice. It is concerned with well-known doctrines which are not readily translated into prayer and practice, and with theology (especially that of St. Thomas Aquinas) which is so often dismissed as 'academic' but which is really very practical.

Every Christian knows that God made the world and saw that it was very good, that Jesus Christ is both God and man, yet this knowledge seems to get lost between the sanctuary and the street: it even gets forgotten between standing for the Creed and kneeling in prayer. The faithful argue fiercely against their agnostic friends who think that Christian morals are negative, prudish and petty, yet when they confess their own sins they are in danger of making just that mistake.

Many a penitent Christian, manfully fighting temptation, tries equally hard to turn himself into a different person altogether: but St. Thomas clearly teaches (if we listen to him) that Grace is to perfect nature and not destroy it. I, for one, will never fully understand his difficult doctrine of 'analogy,' but at its simplest it means that the mind of God does not necessarily work in exactly the same way as ours: which is very practical indeed.

Author's Preface

This book, then, has arisen out of the spiritual guidance of the faithful, and I hope that it may return to that context : that points of special interest will be talked over with another priest and applied to individual needs. Whatever little value the book may have will be greatly increased in that way, for although there is a common basis for all Christian life and prayer, every soul is unique and I feel sure that no amount of books can compensate for a little sane personal direction.

CONTENTS

I

The Purple Headed Mountain

BOOK-TITLES are difficult to choose, and having spent
fruitless hours trying to think of something appropriate, the
present one came to me, just after a winter drive over the
Welsh hills, while Mrs. Alexander's wonderful hymn was
being sung in church :

> The purple headed mountain,
>   The river running by,
> The sunset and the morning,
>   That brightens up the sky ;—
> All things bright and beautiful,
>   All creatures great and small,
> All things wise and wonderful,
>   The Lord God made them all.

The fact that I should have been attending to more important things at that time, that my thoughts were wandering
and that my devotion was pretty tepid, only makes this title
more fitting than ever. Because it puts such failings in their
proper place and defies that tense mock-pietism which is
one of the things I hope this book will help to overthrow.
Apart from that, the title, in its context, hints at the three
fundamental themes which will be treated from various
angles : Prayer, Penitence, and Creation.

Ever since Moses talked with God on Sinai, the idea of
scaling a mountain has remained the classic analogy for the
spiritual pilgrimage, and our first theme is best illustrated
by taking it quite literally. The most obvious thing about
climbing mountains is that it is hard work, demanding dis-

cipline, strength, courage, skill, and above all, stamina;
stamina to plod on, step by step, when the immediate pros-
pect looks dull, uninviting or even dangerous. That all this
applies to Christian living and prayer has been said often
enough before, but we must not forget the other side of the
picture : spiritual mountaineering can be adventurous and
exhilarating, by the grace of God it frequently is, but only
because of our day to day, step by step, disciplined plod.

This brings us to the question of ascetical theology and
spiritual direction. Ascetical theology is the practical doctrine of prayer, its techniques, methods and the disciplines
which help to support and nurture it. Spiritual direction is
its application, by one skilled in this doctrine, to the personal needs of individual people. It all adds up to a science
of co-operation with grace, of using the grace which God
gives us, not only in the fight against temptation and sin,
but in the positive development of those spiritual gifts and
human graces which God bestows far more generously than
we sometimes suppose. I am afraid that the plea : 'I am
not a very "spiritual" person, I have no "gifts"' is more
likely to be sloth than humility, and it is not so far from
blasphemy for it is calling God a miser. Remember the
parable of the pounds (Luke 19 : 12–27) : we may have but
one talent but that is to be doubled not buried. It is also
commonly argued that this ascetical theory, all this method,
technique and discipline, is artificial and unnecessary : why
not pray to God naturally and simply? The plain answer
is why not climb Everest naturally and simply? In neither
case would we get very far, and if by some fluke we got
half-way up the mountain, unaided by knowledge and
technique, we should find ourselves in a very precarious
position. Plainly we need guidance and the best sort is that
supplied by a personal mountain guide.

But in all charity, honest pastoral charity, I do not think that this attitude is caused by culpable spiritual sloth so much as by misunderstanding of what words like 'spiritual,' 'spirituality,' and 'prayer,' really mean. According to St. Augustine, and nearly every one else who followed him, one way in which we are made in the image of God is that we are indivisible trinities of spirit, mind and body. Ideally, spiritual activity, or prayer, perfectly controls reason, which in turn perfectly controls physical appetites and passions. Sin makes none of these things bad, but it upsets the harmony between them. So it is not merely pious but logical to say that only prayer can restore this harmony, only prayer can fully develop a human being because it cannot be divorced from intellectual and bodily needs.

St. Thomas Aquinas says the same thing more positively and more optimistically. He insists as strongly as St. Augustine that man is an integrated being who cannot be split up into body, mind, soul, spirit and so on, prayer is again seen as the proper activity of the whole man. 'Spirituality' does not mean abstract 'religiousness' but the fullest and most perfect *human* development. St. Thomas goes on to teach that, in spite of sin, all men and women are naturally inclined towards their final glory, every one tends towards his or her own perfection, every one is 'potentially' a saint just as every acorn is 'potentially' an oak. If, according to divine providence, it is right for a particular man and woman to be married, then I think St. Thomas would agree that her acceptance of his proposal would constitute 'spiritual progress,' because bodies guided by reason guided by prayer, that is complete personalities, would have reached a decision in accord with the will of God and conducive to their final fulfilment in glory. Thus, in spite of a certain ambiguity, 'spiritual' is the right word to denote total, balanced human progress towards our final glory in heaven, because prayer, in its widest sense, is the key to such progress. 'Spirituality,' then, is simply the art of living, the art of being human, fully, deeply, and perfectly. Plainly it has nothing to do with dreary introspection : in these days especially we must constantly remind ourselves that the true Gospel is concerned not so much with human improvement but with the glory of God. Spiritual life is our total response to that supreme fact.

You cannot climb any worth-while mountain alone. The job demands a team, roped together in the most intimate fellowship, all dependent on each other. We are all unique individuals, but we can only develop through common discipline ; and this is only another way of putting two great Christian doctrines : the vision of God, our final glory, is a corporate experience, because individual Christians can never be dissociated from the Body of Christ.

This particular analogy, however, stresses our membership of a local team : our parish, village, factory or town, which is the sphere of our 'spiritual,' that is all-embracing, life. And we must assume that God has placed us where we are for a special purpose, a 'spiritual,' redemptive purpose : he has given us a job. So next time we doubt our Christian usefulness, next time we deny any 'spiritual' gifts, let us meditate on the fact that God is unlikely to make silly appointments.

Our second general theme presents itself because the mountain we hope to climb is 'purple headed.' We must bear in mind that the Christian life is basically the same all the year round and that it is only particular emphases which vary with the Church's seasons. The Lenten emphasis is penitential, of which the liturgical colour is purple. So we are especially concerned with a penitential mountain and again I think the analogy helps to enlighten us. The whole idea of the climb is to get somewhere. It implies movement towards a destination. To use the technical term it is 'teleological' which is the principle of Christian morals. Sin is not so much disobedience to an arbitrary set of negative rules but that which impedes the development of our potential glory. Sins are like unnecessary burdens which hinder our climb, temptation is the obstacle in our path which is to be overcome in order that we may go on: up to the summit, up towards God. We cannot, in other words, divorce morals from ascetics, goodness from prayer. No one has ever climbed a mountain by sitting at its base and just being good, and I see no logical reason to believe that any one has ever reached heaven by similar methods.

The purple headed mountain is a glorious thing, a sublimely beautiful thing, and if we manage to get to the top two things happen. First we can *see*. We can see clearly for miles round, we see a whole new panorama of intoxicating beauty, we see the world around us as we cannot possibly see it from the valleys and plains. Penitence means knowledge, of ourselves, of the world, and of God, and knowledge leads to love. Penitence clarifies our vision, it helps us to develop that insight into the ways of God with things and people which the text-books call 'wisdom.' Penitence is thus the first quality to look for in a spiritual guide, and I think this is what St. Teresa meant when she preferred the direction of a learned man to that of a holy one. Of course she did not see these qualities as mutually exclusive! Nor do I think she confined learning to theological knowledge, although she regarded that as of great importance. I think she meant that wisdom or discernment which is a gift of the Holy Spirit and which seems always to be born of, and to thrive upon, penitence. So our quest for penitence, far from being a negative, introverted, unhealthy thing, is a search for truth every bit as creative as the search for truth by scholars and scientists. It is an essential part of the map of the spiritual mountain, part of the technique needed for a successful and vigorous climb.

According to the classic analogy, on the top of the mountain is God. We speak glibly about 'recollection' or of 'the presence of God,' or of 'being near our Lord.' Truly to be with God is the ultimate glory, to live in his presence is our day to day aim, but if the saints can stand before him because of their perfection, we can do so only because of our penitence. So penitence is the key to our present foretaste of final glory, it is the one thing needful for all that is implied by 'Holy Communion.' 'If we say that we have no sin, we deceive ourselves, and the *truth* is not in us' (1 John 1 : 8). To say we have no sin is to be not so much wicked as blind, to be vaguely conscious of sinfulness without facing it is not to be strong but cowardly: to be impenitent is to be half alive. But the attainment of penitence is not easy, we have to plod up the mountain to its purple headed peak: only then can we see, and rejoice in our vision.

The third general theme of this book is the most important of all, because it underlies a proper approach to the other two and is more neglected than either. There is nothing quite so solid and unmistakable as a mountain, yet how often do we fail to see its significance in the classic analogy? For a mountain is an awesome, wonderful, spectacular part of God's *creation*, and our title comes from a hymn to creation, which, like the *Benedicite*, is both gloriously simple and wonderfully rich. Both hymns are associated with the deep religious qualities of children, simplicity, purity, integrity, wonder; and I always think that the hymnal which primly states that *All things bright and beautiful* is 'also suitable for adults' deserves first prize for comic understatement.

Christian life, inspired by Christian prayer, is Christian doctrine translated into action, but lately we seem to have forgotten the first sentence of the Creed. Our prayer, the mainspring of everything else, has become detached from the doctrine of creation; which makes our devotion anæmic and shallow, our penitence prudish, and our faith without joy. Our prayers have become moralistic appendages to life instead of its central power, our worship gets more and more 'religious' instead of our lives bubbling over with worship. It may help to overcome this state of affairs if we first try to discover its causes, and I do not believe we shall get very far by blaming secular trends or by accusing the Church of being out of date and disinterested in social and economic problems, or by saying that we are too much concerned with theology and not enough with practice. There may be some truth in all that, but I do not think it is the real reason. In fact I would be inclined to argue that the practical influence of the Church upon the world is less effective than it might be because we are not theological enough : we have forgotten the *doctrine* of creation. The deeper reasons for this, I suggest, are twofold, and curiously, they are associated with the opposite poles of our Anglican tradition.

In the first place we cannot quite get rid of our innate English puritanism, which in its theological sense means the quest for 'pure spirituality' and a consequent suspicion of the human body, its needs and appetites, and all the creatures which meet them. Our prayer becomes tainted with that error against which St. Thomas so strongly warns : we try to be angels instead of sanctified human beings, we do not expect grace to perfect our nature but to change it into something different. Our idea of Jesus Christ is orthodox when we stand for the Creed and heresy when we kneel in prayer; it becomes Apollinarian, for we cannot face up to his full, perfect, eternal *humanity*. He becomes a vague ideal, a shadowy symbol, a devout image, but not a *man* with human appetites, passions, needs and temptations, a man to whom the created world is the proper and necessary environment.

If this puritanism is associated with the 'Protestant' element in our religion, the second error comes from the 'Catholic' side; it is what I must consider to be an unhealthy dabbling in 'mysticism.' Let us be quite clear that mysticism is an essential and glorious part of the Christian gospel, but in any age the Church's true mystics are a very small minority. Most of us have to serve God in humbler ways, and the one practical value of mysticism to us is that which Dr. Mascall pointed out in last year's book in this series (*Grace and Glory*); it reminds us that, in whatever state we are, absolute glory, the vision, love, and perfect praise of God in heaven, is our final end, and we must never be content with anything less. The constant danger of ascetical theology, dealing with the methods and techniques proper to the mountain's lower slopes, is to confuse the means with the end. The mystics remind us that however long the journey, however remote the summit, however shrouded in the mystical clouds, we must ever recognize by faith that God is really there. The danger is that mystical theology is a highly technical subject with a very esoteric vocabulary of its own, consisting largely of negative terms associated with the sixth century writings of the pseudo-Dionysius. To the uninitiated, phrases like 'the dark night of sense,' 'the cloud of unknowing,' 'distraction from creatures,' sound utterly world-renouncing. God's creation is made to sound evil, or at least a hindrance, which is not quite what the mystics mean, and which is totally irrelevant to the huge majority of us who are not mystics and never will be. For the slothful it is a great temptation to mis-interpret the mystics in a cheap and vulgar search for spiritual thrills, to misuse them to find excuse for neglecting proper worldly responsibilities and for avoiding the humbler disciplines of everyday Christian living. As Gerald Vann writes in *Morals and Man:* 'There is a policy of Get Rich Quick in the spiritual as well as the worldly sphere; and it is ultimately anti-christian.' (Fontana edition, p. 53.) You cannot reach the mountain's summit by taking a running jump at it.

Those, I believe, are the deeper reasons for present neg-lect of the doctrine of creation, which in turn is responsible for a divorce between devotion and work, prayer, and morals, the Church and the world. These divisions cannot be healed by superficial, or artificial, means, because 'Christian principles' are not statutes written in a book, but the action of the Incarnate Redeemer working through his Body the Church. If the three saints we are to meet in chapter III were exhorted to 'relate religion to life' they would reply, with some bewilderment, that religion *is* related to life, not because of the latest Church Campaign, but because of the Incarnation. If this divorce is apparent to-day it does not mean that we are not achieving aims but that we are failing to face facts. We have to realize that a slum street is not an abstract social problem but a concrete thing, that sin is not merely defiance of moral theory but a practical misuse of creation, that prayer and penitence are not holy feelings but an inspired attempt to understand the meaning of the created world around us.

The Purple Headed Mountain

Here, then, are the three main themes of this little book, the three characteristics of the purple headed mountain : ascetical doctrine which makes prayer positive and vital, penitence, the Lenten emphasis, and the doctrine of creation, so neglected and yet so necessary to true Christian life. Let us start our climb.

II

Obedience and Love

ALL Christian teachers agree about the first two steps in our spiritual climb, although they present them in different ways. There is the 'Purgative Way' in which we are mainly concerned with overcoming our sins, and the 'Illuminative Way' when we are enlightened by grace in the cultivation of virtue. There is discursive meditation when we struggle to understand our faith, and affective prayer wherein we become conscious of the love of God and enjoy our response to it. Our own great teacher, Walter Hilton, speaks of 'reforming in faith' followed by 'reforming in feeling.' But, for our present purpose, the most practical form of this teaching is given by William of St. Thierry, the friend and biographer of St. Bernard, who begins with 'necessary obedience,' expressing faith and hope, which leads into 'loving obedience' qualified by charity.

By obeying the ascetical principles which arise out of the living experience of the Church, we are led to love our Lord in a sensible, or conscious, way. By doing what we are told without quite knowing why, except through faith and hope, we come to obey Christ in his Church because we love obeying him. All of which is common sense : small children obey their parents 'necessarily,' because they have to, even if they cannot understand why they must clean their teeth, and tell the truth and not walk all over the house in muddy shoes. But eventually, because of this 'necessary obedience,' they come to see how wise their parents are, how concerned for their welfare, and how valuable all this discipline has been; they continue to obey, but freely and lovingly. They have been—literally—'well brought up.'

'Necessary obedience' consists not in vague moral tenets but in a disciplined acceptance of, and co-operation with, grace; by a systematic use of the sacraments and prayer in loyalty to the Church's experience and teaching, for only so armed is it possible to acquire love, virtue and practical Christian wisdom. William of St. Thierry is never content to inspire us with good intentions and pious feelings, he tells us very clearly and very bluntly exactly what we have to do. He does not tell us to say a few prayers and we shall *feel* better, he says do this for six months and we shall *be* better. He does not say try a little meditation and hope for the best, he says do this and the Church guarantees that it will work.

What, then, is 'necessary obedience' in practice? The Church has never been in any doubt that the basic pattern of Christian life rests on three fundamental and inter-related things: the Holy Eucharist, our ordinary means of grace and the centre of all Christian life, the channel of redemption for ourselves and all creation; the Church's formal Office, the continuous praise of God by, and through, the Body of Christ, and our share in the eternal adoration of heaven; and our own unique, personal devotion according to our particular gifts and temperament.

There is nothing arbitrary or artificial about this for it clearly comes from the New Testament: the Eucharist instituted at the Last Supper; all kinds of personal devotion by people as different as Zacchaeus and St. Peter, as Martha and Mary, and the Lord's Prayer, the first 'set prayer' or 'Office' of the whole Church. And it has developed ever since, especially by St. Basil, St. Benedict, later by the Friars Minor, and in a very special way by the Anglican

24

Church. But although it has developed, according to needs and circumstances, the basic pattern is unchanged and unchangeable.

I have always been surprised that this practical, living pattern of prayer is so seldom seen as a test for the orthodoxy of a particular communion. That a church is truly Catholic and Apostolic is argued with reference to its Creeds, its Ministry, its use of the Bible, its sacraments and so on, all of which of course are of great importance, but the daily *use* of this universal threefold pattern seems to me to be a test of equal significance. It is especially important to see this Rule as one integrated thing, one basis for the truly 'spiritual,' or completely human, life. We are not dealing with three separate, or separable, things, but with a unity. So the high churchman who stresses the Eucharist and belittles the Office, the low churchman who likes Matins and Evensong at the expense of the Eucharist, and the free churchman who emphasizes personal devotion against formal corporate worship—'set prayers'—are all making the same basic error. They are all too concerned with 'services' and not concerned enough with total Christian life based on the Church's Rule.

The Anglican form of this system is embodied in the Book of Common Prayer, which orders the Holy Eucharist on all Sundays and certain other festivals, a twofold daily Office, and private devotion according to personal needs and abilities. The great Anglican contribution to the development of this Rule is that it solidly unites the whole Church : unlike the Roman Communion, or Eastern Orthodoxy, Anglicanism binds together bishop, priest, Religious, and layman, by the same Rule, the same offices, the same book. That is why we have usually managed to avoid that horrible gulf between priesthood and laity which has played havoc throughout Christian history. There is a book by an eminent Roman Catholic writer which is dedicated to 'The Laity' whom he describes as 'God's Little People.' This writer is renowned for his great pastoral love and wisdom, and I have no doubt that his dedication is meant humbly and charitably, but to me, and I think most Anglicans, it is nauseating. Priest and layman are not the same, but they make one solid family in Christ, although the implications of this are not always realized.

Devout people sometimes come to me, especially at the beginning of Lent, and ask if I will 'give them a Rule.' This often means will I help with the personal and variable part of their prayer, which is ordinary spiritual guidance. But I am afraid that some of the faithful expect, and even hope for, one of those wretched little lists of innumerable trivialities that so often, and so mistakenly, are called 'Rules.' The blunt fact is that neither myself, nor any other priest, nor even William of St. Thierry, has any right to alter the fundamental Rule which we are all given by the Church itself : Eucharist, office, devotion. We might sometimes have to alter or modify the details, but we cannot change the structure. It is this, and this only, that constitutes 'necessary obedience' to Jesus Christ as members of his Body.

I have already written a frightening number of words, in various places, in an attempt to explain just how, and why, this threefold plan works, and works so effectively : how it gives practical expression to our faith in the Most Holy Trinity, in the one God who is Father Almighty, utterly majestic and transcendent, who is the God-Man, Christ our Lord and Redeemer, who is the Holy Ghost, the indwelling Comforter, immanently active in the very depths of our being. I have tried to show how it balances and integrates our corporate membership of Christ's Church with our unique individuality, how it relates objective worship to personal petition, how it assures our spiritual growth by keeping our prayer healthy. Still more important, I have tried to explain why this fundamental loyalty is the greatest act of Christian witness to the world, and the basis of all evangelism.

In the 87th *Tract,* Isaac Williams wrote : 'If we were to judge from Holy Scripture, of what were the best means of promoting Christianity in the world, we should say obedience ; and if we were asked the second, we should say obedience ; and if we were asked the third, we should say obedience.' So emphatic a pronouncement must mean more than a vague attempt at a 'decent moral life.' It can only mean what William of St. Thierry meant : the disciplined participation in the continuous rhythm of the Church's life, the constant co-operation with grace in the Mystical Body.

I cannot repeat all these arguments here. It must suffice to exhort the reader to try the experiment for himself. But I must add one or two practical points about the daily Office, which, after all, is the only thing likely to cause any difficulty to any one keen enough to bother with this sort of book at all.

First, the Office will really help Eucharistic worship and private prayer, it is the perfect preparation for both. Secondly, the very perfection of life is the perfect praise of God, but it is useless to order people 'to praise God.' Let us face the fact that to most of us most of the time God is vague and remote. Occasionally grace may stir our hearts and minds to true praise but that is a precarious possibility to bank on. The Church's Office is perfect because it is Christ's prayer to the Father, the saints enter into it eternally, and we are privileged to enter into it occasionally, twice a day, by virtue of our membership of Christ. So when we recite the Offices, our Lord is helping us, making us, praise God as perfectly as we are able. He is lifting the whole thing out of the perilous sphere of our own moods, feelings, and emotions. We shall get to value it so much, sometimes it may be a burden and a bore, *but that does not matter:* we are praising God and loving God because Christ is making up for our weakness, and we are being obedient.

Thirdly, regular Offices save us from that awful, scrupulous, mock-pious tension which comes from too much reliance on our own feelings and emotions. The Office is a wonderful thing to fall back on, as an honest, down-to-earth, Christian job of work, when things get difficult and dull. Fourthly, the technique of the Office, the effort to *give* praise to God, almost to throw the psalms and canticles towards him, outwardly, in utter self-forgetfulness, is the supreme weapon against morbid introspection, 'self-culture,' or religious egotism.

It must now be admitted that our present Offices, admirable as they might have been for the seventeenth century, need a good deal of revision to meet the needs and contingencies of the twentieth. If modification is really necessary, I suggest that the lessons be omitted, not because the Bible is unimportant—far from it, as we shall see later—but because I very much doubt if the middle of an Office is the best place for its study or meditation : not to mention that my personal opinion of the current Lectionary is quite unprintable. But offer to God at least the collect, psalms and canticles; regularly, daily, selflessly, without fuss or tension, in church, at home, in the train or on the bus. Together with Holy Communion and private devotion, it will be far more worth while than innumerable little rules, fasts, mortifications and popular devotions. Let us get down to religion and up that mountain, let us stop playing at it.

Whenever parish priests write or teach in this way they face a dilemma. I am sure we all realize that this kind of discipline is much easier for us than for busy lay people, it is our basic work which does not have to be squeezed into another different job. We are naturally reluctant to risk overburdening the loyal laity, but if we adopt the easier course of failing to insist on these *necessary,* fundamental things, then we are getting dangerously near to the horrid heresy of 'God's Little People': the idea that the laity should not be taken too seriously and cannot be expected to be spiritually adult. This latter approach is wholly opposed to Anglican tradition, and to me it is abominable: so at least forgive me for taking the former line. Because of canonical (or necessary) obligation, every priest comes to know by experience how valuable the Office is and what a vital part it plays in his own spiritual development. This kind of exhortation is not a question of laying a burden on the layman but of inviting him to share in an adult Christian technique of proved worth.

I believe, moreover, that, in view of the magnificent labours laypeople give to parochial and diocesan affairs, the 'burden' of the Church's Rule is a little exaggerated. I think the real trouble is due to a lack of ascetical theology: it is not that the Anglican Rule is too difficult, or takes up too much time, but that we are not really convinced of its proven value, of its necessity if the Church is to fulfil its real job. We are too inclined to interpret the worth of our prayer in terms of feeling and emotion, lack of theology makes practical 'Church work' seem so much more worth while than the recitation of 'set prayers.' But 'spirituality' includes both, and the value of practical work depends on the Church's continuous life of praise : only thus can practical work be Christian.

There is a healthy reaction against the sort of 'devotion' which isolates itself from the work-a-day world, but the answer is not to stop praying but to pray in a different spirit, more efficiently and theologically. For centuries personal Anglican devotion was centred on the Prayer Book Offices. The later Tractarians introduced a whole new series of popular devotions, and new methods and techniques of mental prayer. I remain doubtful if, on balance, we have gained very much by them. If this new devotion and method adds richness and variety to our religious experience, then the gain is considerable, but if they are substituted for the solid foundation, if they tend to undermine our fundamental ascetical system, then the position is very serious. Devotion, affective experience, sensible love for God, can only be won through necessary obedience.

William of St. Thierry saw the essential connection between obedience and love, thus lifting love from the morass of emotionalism so often associated with it, especially in its religious context : which again is only common sense. A man surely loves his wife, if he loves her truly, both 'affectively' and 'necessarily.' He loves her in the intimate union of marriage, passionately, devotedly and romantically, yet he is still expressing that love by washing the dishes, chopping wood and getting the coal. There is something very wrong with the romantic husband who takes his wife for moonlit walks, buys her flowers, and refuses to lift a finger to help clean out the drains. That is very much the position of the Christian who indulges in a lot of frilly devotions but jibs at regular discipline. A further aspect of 'necessary' love is that the husband should go out to work to provide for his family and if real love is there, it is automatically carried over into work and life; everything is controlled and coloured by it. There is something equally horrible about the husband who thinks he meets all his responsibilities by handing over the weekly pay-packet. Those who interpret their 'practical religion' as good honest work for society, or even for 'the church,' without being bothered with sacraments and prayers, are unpleasantly near just that position.

III

Creation and Prayer

THE link between prayer and the doctrine of creation is the key to practical Christian life in the world. It offers a relation which carries the influence of our faith out into the market-place, it provides us with the most subtle, and probably most effective, of all methods of Christian witness, and it forms another safeguard against that error which packs 'spirituality' into a nasty little ecclesiastical box tied up with pietistical red-tape.

Christian history shows four stages through which this relation has been worked out. Only the final stage is wholly satisfactory, but each makes an important contribution, and, as so often happens with theology, passing errors have their value in bringing out the final truth more clearly.

Up to the time of St. Bernard of Clairvaux, the Church had been forced to insist upon the essential goodness of the natural world. Despite the plain statement, repeated seven times in the first chapter of the Bible, that God had made it and 'saw that it was good,' the first thousand years of Christian history were bedevilled by the idea that God was wrong. During this period, Greek and Oriental ideas about the evil of matter and the goodness of 'spirit' were always trying to insinuate themselves into Christian theology, and some of the early 'ascetics'—in the popular but inaccurate sense of that term—regrettably succumbed to this heretical influence. But on the whole, the Church stood firmly by the book of Genesis.

In the writings of saints like Augustine, Ambrose, Hilary

and Bernard, we come across glorious outbursts of praise for God's wonderful creation, and there are fine passages and poems extolling the beauty of the natural world manifesting the majesty of its Creator. But here a different dualism creeps in. These saints teach about prayer, discipline and the sacraments, and they all firmly insist that God's world is good, but there is no very clear connection between the two. Their hymns to creation sound like some of our devotional sermons: we come away edified and inspired but without having been told anything very practical; when the uplift wears off we have little idea what we are supposed to do about it.

The second stage comes with the teaching of the school of St. Victor, more especially, for our purpose, of St. Hugh. According to his teaching, the universe is *symbolic* of the mind of God, the world is like a gigantic book in which every creature, every created thing, is as a word written by God. Thus the world does not simply manifest God in a general, almost intellectual, way, as it does in the earlier poems, but in a much more direct and detailed way. If we contemplate some single thing, a flower, rock or tree, it will give us some particular knowledge of God, so the more we know about the world the more we know about God, and, following St. Augustine, to know God is to love him. To St. Hugh there can be no conflict between science and religion because they are practically the same thing: he would have said that our nuclear physicists were really making meditations, they were but making further enquiries into the mind of the Creator by examining his works.

The importance of this is that our prayer, worship, devotion and love, all our religion, is based upon, and begins with, creation, with being in the world and getting to know, understand and love, material things. It is the religious counterpart to the philosophical axiom that all knowledge starts with sense-experience. To St. Hugh and the Victorines, our Christian pilgrimage does not begin with kneeling down and closing our eyes but with standing up and opening them very wide, much wider than we generally do. This is what modern writers call 'the first form of contemplation,' the purposeful, devout contemplation of God's creatures, thence the attainment of a harmony with them, of seeing ourselves as parts of God's good and unified design. The practical value of this is what the textbooks call 'habitual recollection,' the habit of recognizing the divine presence everywhere, of seeing all things, including ourselves, as created and sustained from moment to moment by the love of God. This habitual sense of God's omnipresence in things, of their, and our, absolute dependence on him, this childlike sense of *wonder,* is one of the most potent weapons against the root sin of pride.

But there is one serious snag in this system. Creation, far from being an evil impediment, is shown to be essential to the life of prayer, but it is not really good because it is not 'really' anything; it is no more than 'symbolic.' The 'book of creation' is not read very easily, its message is not always clear, and St. Hugh explains this by a metaphor which was universally popular in the ascetical thinking of his age; we only see creation as if reflected in a mirror. But the reflection of something in a mirror, though an identical image, is not that thing itself. So the Victorines foreshadow that idealist philosophy which was to be a nuisance to Christian thought in England in the eighteenth century. In some ways, in fact, this system is not unlike that of Bishop Berkeley who taught, to put it rather too simply, that things only existed 'in the eye of the beholder.'

ultimate purpose of which is perfectly to join in the adoration of the Creator : all things in their own order, in their own special way, according to their own characteristics.

As G. K. Chesterton so delightfully treats of it in his study of the Angelic Doctor (*St. Thomas Aquinas,* Chap. 6), this great doctrine of creation firmly insists that eggs are not symbols, nor our sisters, nor embryonic hens, nor the by-products of a poultry farm, nor complexes of sense-data : eggs are, indubitably and unquestionably, eggs. And what is even more important, men are men. Our prayers have to be the best possible kind of human prayers, our lives must be good human lives. So it is not only useless but sinful to try to be 'spiritual' like the angels because we are not angels, we never shall be angels, and we were never supposed to be angels : we are supposed to be glorified men and women. Further, we are supposed to be ourselves, perfected and sanctified, but not changed into somebody else : grace perfects nature. And, of course, it is impossible to be ourselves, men and women as God has created us, except in, and with a proper relation to, the whole creation which is our necessary environment.

This is the mountain we are to climb and St. Thomas gives us some very important information about its structure, which helps us with our technique. This ordered hierarchy of Creation truly lead us to our goal : base to apex, inanimate matter to God. All creatures are real, important and necessary to our journey, but the essential distinctions between them remain. In some respects apes resemble men, in some respects men resemble angels, but always eggs are eggs, apes are apes, men are men, angels are angels. We cannot logically argue, or deduce facts from the behaviour of one group to that of another. More particularly, we cannot logically understand God by direct inference from his creatures : we cannot say because good men think thus, therefore God must think thus. But what we cannot do by logic we can by analogy; in other words we may approach God through his creatures by jumps of faith, faith gives us hints about God's glory because of the glory of creation, but we must always keep his transcendence in devout remembrance. By immanence God is in all things, by his transcendence he is absolutely remote from them, his glory so far exceeds any experience this world can know or give.

Let us remember here, in parentheses as it were, that it is the daily Office, shared with saints and angels, offered in and through our Lord, objectively, selflessly *given* to God the Father Almighty : it is this daily discipline that ever reminds us of God transcendent and saves us from that weak sentimentality which must follow an over-emphasis on God's 'closeness' and 'friendship.'

Our mountain then, according to St. Thomas, is not so much a gentle incline as a series of ledges, steps indeed but steps just too big for a comfortable, logical walk. We have to live with creation, watch and contemplate creation, but we have to take a series of jumps from one thing to another, and from all to God : jumps into the dark, jumps of devotion, jumps of faith, jumps of hope, and jumps of love.

That, as simply as I can put it, is roughly and absurdly briefly what St. Thomas means by 'analogy.' But all that concerns us is this doctrine's ordinary pastoral implications, which may become a little clearer if we consider two or three practical examples.

If the three saints we have been considering looked at a daisy, Hugh of St. Victor would immediately recognize that God made it and kept it alive by love, that God was somehow 'in' it and we could seek him through it : the 'first form of contemplation' or 'habitual recollection,' all of which is excellent. But it would only be a symbol, St. Hugh would ask what it meant and he might just possibly conclude that it signified that our Lady in Heaven wore a delicate white veil and a golden crown. No doubt that is the attitude from which a good many popular names for flowers arose—Madonna lilies, Marigold, our Lady's Tears and so on—it is the idea that thunder means that God is angry, and of course it is carrying symbolism too far. It is a similar error to the crudely allegorical interpretations of the Bible in earlier ages.

St. Francis would just love the daisy, he could easily kiss it, or even preach it a little sermon. He would be at one with it and would no doubt find God in it in some mystical way. St. Thomas would love it too, not as a divine symbol, nor as obviously related to him, not as a pattern of our Lady's appearance, but as a daisy. He would see a reflection of God's glory in it and would himself adore God in his way as the daisy did in its way : he would thank God and glorify and praise God because of this glorious daisyhood.

Supposing our saintly trio walked along a slum street ? Perhaps Hugh of St. Victor would start to analyse the causes why here God's creation seemed symbolic of sin rather than glory : the deep meditation of the *real* Christian sociologist, St. Francis would go on loving, people, dirt, garbage, lice and all ; and no doubt his sanctity would go a long way to redeem them. Only St. Thomas, I think, would consider tearing it all down and building something better : here are creatures that are not fulfilling their essential purpose, they do not glorify God, they do not help men and women to achieve their proper end. I do not think any of the three are wrong, and they all offer very practical pastoral teaching to the twentieth century.

Lastly, let us suppose they were presented with a glass of wine. St. Hugh would first admire its colour and bouquet—symbol—then he would consider the mind of God who arranged all the natural processes by which it was produced; here is the religious scientist. And he would surely ask *why* God arranged all these complex reactions especially in their relation to the human organism of body and mind: which is a very important question to ask. St. Francis would love it without wanting it. St. Thomas would end by drinking it because that, primarily, is what it is for, that is its true end, and he would give God thanks for unique vinousness as well as for unique daisyhood. None would ever risk getting drunk: St. Hugh because it dulled the mind and senses, St. Francis because it would be extravagant, and St. Thomas because it would be unreasonable—which are three very good reasons. The drunkard is not one who is too fond of himself and of wine, but one with nothing like enough reverence for either. As we shall see in chapter V, all seven capital sins are sins against creation.

To sum up so far: our 'spiritual life' is our total life in and with all creation, but it will only grow and flourish if all is sanctified by the Eucharist, offered to God Transcendent through the Office; and consolidated by our personal prayer.

IV

Self-examination and Penitence

LIKE all Christian virtues, love, humility, faith and so on, penitence is volitional rather than emotional; it is a question of facing facts rather than of stirring up feelings. This does not deny the value of affective penitence, when we are moved to contrition by seeing the heinousness of sin against the divine love manifested in the Passion and Cross of our Blessed Lord. But such devotion is usually the fruit of more mundane fact-facing, of a whole life of disciplined prayer aided by sane, cool, self-examination. Real contrition presents us with the same difficulty as pure praise : one cannot just 'do it.' Because of our frailty and concupiscence we are unable to see just what sin means to God, our sensitivity must be allowed to grow with the continuous spiritual struggle. But as the Office helps especially to develop our ability to praise, so self-examination helps to deepen our sense of contrition. It must therefore be taken seriously, as indeed it seems to be to judge by the multitude of little manuals which continue to pour from the presses. Such guides obviously vary in quality and usefulness but I think most of them suffer from no less than five general weaknesses.

First, they are abstract : self-examination becomes a pious exercise divorced from Christian life, it is the same mistake as thinking of the Eucharist, the Office and private prayer as three isolated things. As I have tried to explain elsewhere, self-examination is closely linked with petition, which may, indeed, be the best form of it. If you want a new motor-car then pray for one, ask God about it, and he will immediately ask why you want it. If you want to impress the neighbours, or if it is for self-indulgent pleasure, or for pure vanity, then you will be forced to admit it to Christ more certainly than to a book asking 'Have I been envious? have I been covetous? have I been self-centred?'

Secondly, some of these manuals are negative because they forget that Christian morals are always 'teleological': they are concerned only with the attainment of an end, not with 'being good.' As Dr. Kirk taught so clearly, sin is validly defined as that which impedes spiritual progress (*Some Principles of Moral Theology,* p. 228). In other words, we cannot divorce moral from ascetical theology, behaviour from prayer, prayer from living, for if we do, we tend to make God into a kind of over-sized schoolmaster laying down a lot of little rules for no apparent purpose. Thus our self-examination manual degenerates into one of those dreary lists of questions, some of which are ludicrous and many more irrelevant. What is right is that which helps us up God's mountain, what is wrong impedes the climb, so St. Thomas sums up the matter by saying that 'actions which are contrary to the natural moral law are not wrong because God prohibits them; they are prohibited by God because they are wrong.' Once that is taken seriously we see that self-examination is no morbid introspection but an objective quest for truth; a serious piece of research into the truth about God and creation which is linked up with our journey towards himself.

The third weakness is a tendency to nurture what an American professor of moral theology calls the 'schoolgirl conscience.' This is divisible into two errors which arise from a conscience immature and untrained: first a whole new list of taboos and conventions which are mistaken for sins, then a total lack of perspective about real sin. The former mistake underlies those diabolical little questions like 'Have I always been devout and reverent at Holy Communion? Have I allowed my mind to wander during prayer?' If the answer to this nonsense is 'no' then you have not made your Communion very often and you have said precious few prayers. I do not think 'diabolical' is too strong a word, for it is precisely this sort of thing that panders to an unholy tension, turns God into an ogre, and drowns the soul in pride because all the normal frailties and shortcomings of human nature are discounted. The result is the fatal practice of praying only when we feel like it, putting us at the mercy of scrupulosity, pietism, and practically everything else unhealthy. The latter mistake is made by those who gaily forget about their Communion on Ascension Day and indignantly refuse to play golf on Sunday afternoon: it is all disastrously back to front. It is like the schoolgirl who sneaks off with half a glass of cooking sherry and a cigarette, firmly believing that she has sounded the very depths of depravity; while her habitual pride, hatred and jealousy pass unnoticed.

What is happening here is far more serious than these trivial examples suggest, for it is no less than a full rejection of St. Thomas' teaching about analogy. The 'schoolgirl conscience' argues straight from its own moral emotion, tied to the conventions of the narrowest of coteries, to the eternal mind of God. In pastoral practice it is frequently encountered in the attitude 'I am quite sure God objects to this, and I am quite sure he will not mind that.' Bluntly 'men think like this, therefore God must think like this,' which, as St. Thomas insists very strongly, just does not necessarily follow.

Conscience must be trained, it has to be guided by the

objective light of moral theology; and that brings us to the fourth point. Which moral theology?

We cannot argue directly from the human moral consciousness to the mind of God, but of course there is one all-important exception to this rule. The human mind, conscience and practice of Jesus Christ is exactly the mind and will of God. Constant meditation on the life of Jesus himself, habitual recollection of him, life fully in his presence; this is the supreme method of self-examination. But we cannot achieve this immediately or adequately, there must still be some external guide, some standard or system by which we can examine ourselves; in other words some moral theology. Both needs are combined when we consider that not only individuals like ourselves, but the whole Church throughout its history, has constantly meditated upon the person and life of our Lord. Moral theology is but the codification of all this experience, and for self-examination the classical outcome is the list of 'seven capital sins.'

The fourth mistake is when the capital sins become 'academic' theology, unrelated to real life because unrelated to creation. But this system is not easy to understand, so many of the manuals short circuit the difficulty by using some other scheme of doubtful value except that it is simpler. Sometimes we get an unholy mixture of two or three different schemes, and the result is invariably the same : pages and pages of little questions. The more constructive answer is to retain the capital sins of orthodox tradition, but to try to understand them as practical guides to Christian living, by placing them in the context of both redemption *and* creation, which, when you come to think of them, cannot very well be separated. I once heard an argument between two Churchmen as to whether Godchildren should be specially remembered on their birthdays or on the date of their Baptism. One insisted that the latter, the day of spiritual regeneration, of rebirth in grace, the beginning of redemption, was the more important. The other countered that, although the point was impressive, it was difficult to be baptized until one had been born : so the argument was rightly inconclusive. We shall further consider this relation in the next chapter.

The fifth difficulty relates to the approach to, rather than the content of, this moral theology. Speaking very generally the Council of Trent, meeting from 1545 to 1563, and considering moral theology in great detail, perpetuated the dusty old heresy of dissociating morals from ascetic. Meanwhile our own Caroline Divines were fighting hard against this tendency. The former, therefore, became juridical and to a large extent legalistic, while the latter was more pastoral and devotional. It is very disturbing that to-day Roman Catholic thought is reacting against the post-Tridentine teaching while Anglicanism is in danger of forsaking its own tradition in favour of it.

In classical moral theology, actual sin is divided into 'mortal' and 'venial,' and the three essential characteristics of 'mortal' sin are that it must be serious—a 'big' sin—it must be committed with full knowledge of its sinfulness, and with complete and free surrender of the will. To commit mortal sin we must know that it is seriously wrong and we must do it on purpose. As Dr. Kirk has pointed out (ibid., p. 247), this is a useful distinction for a confessor to keep in the back of his mind, but it is pastorally unreal and may be positively dangerous to ordinary penitents. So Anglican moral theology pastoralizes the distinction into sins, not 'mortal' and 'venial' but of 'malice' and 'infirmity.' To us, therefore, penitence and confession is not a juridical tribunal, a kind of divine law court where justice is dispensed according to the book, but an act of worship, a generous prostration of our complete selves at the foot of the Cross without a lot of intricate distinctions. Anglicans do not, in William Beveridge's great phrase, 'stand upon fine points with God Almighty' : for to try to do so is to forget that God *is* Almighty. Anglicans may confess their sins either privately or sacramentally, but in either case they confess *everything* in complete self-oblation. Penitence is a quest for the whole truth, in which we are guided by deciding if particular sins are due to our frailty, or to natural infirmity, or to positive malice, to plain ill-will. Are we seriously trying to reach God on the mountain top, in spite of a few nasty stumbles, or are we turning our backs to him deliberately?

This approach also helps with some of the doubts arising from modern psychological knowledge. I discount all the extreme 'behaviourist' or 'determinist' theories as un-Christian nonsense. But there may well be truth in those theories which maintain that, although we remain responsible moral beings, although no Christian, aided by grace, can ever commit sin and claim that he 'cannot help it,' factors of environment, temperament, heredity, upbringing and so on, may well have more to do with our behaviour than was once supposed. The effect of this new knowledge on the 'mortal-venial' distinction is to draw the line a little higher, a little more in our favour. It is getting just a little harder to affirm that certain sins of certain people are committed 'with full consent of the will.' For example, there is no doubt that drunkenness is seriously sinful, but if an alcoholic gets drunk it takes a good deal of thought to decide whether his sin is 'mortal' or not. It is clearly different either from a normal man setting out to get drunk or from an undergraduate who takes a little too much at a college party. Such questions can be very complicated, but the important thing is that in all these cases it is not so very difficult for the men concerned to decide whether their fall is due to infirmity or to positive malice against God.

Finally the old legalist distinctions are shown to be unsatisfactory by the fact that all this 'new' psychological knowledge is not so new after all. St. Thomas is quite clear about the 'mortal-venial' distinction, but he is equally aware of the complexity of any 'deliberate' human act. He analyses it into no less than twelve steps or stages, so that one wonders whether, having clearly defined a 'mortal sin,' it is really possible for any one to commit it. But our own William Beveridge has the final answer : we do not stand upon fine points with God, we aim to go out to reach him, to love, praise and adore him. All our sins, big, small, known and unknown, culpable or ignorant, wilful or frail ; all have to go. In confession we do not seek acquittal on the easiest possible terms, we seek God in generous oblation. 'The whole basis of teleological ethics,' writes Gerald Vann, 'is the idea of moral action as the striving after an end to be attained rather than the achievement of conformity to the rule of right.'

Another common, and I think unnecessary, pastoral worry is the Thomist doctrine that mortal sin 'cuts off' the soul from God. This creates many difficulties for St. Thomas himself, from which he wriggles out very ingeniously. He opposes William of St. Thierry who likens Baptism to Marriage : the twain—the baptized soul and Christ—are one flesh, never to be divorced. Thus 'mortal sin' is not so much an offence which carries the maximum penalty as a very serious marital quarrel, an act of unfaithfulness against Christ to whom we are espoused. This teaching can never be called lax, in a sense it makes mortal sin even worse, and it more readily stirs us to contrition and penitence. We need not go into all the intricacies of the two systems, but it may safely be said that William of St. Thierry is the more pastoral, the more Anglican, nearer to the Caroline virtue of generosity, and of much devotional value. We may freely follow him.

Growing penitence is part of our total spiritual progress, the ultimate test for which is moral theology itself. We are growing in spirit, not when we get more consoling feelings or when our meditations are exciting, but when we commit fewer sins. These, indeed, frequently go together, but we must not mistake the single trustworthy test. But there are, if not infallible tests, then at least further useful signs of growing penitence and maturity of conscience, and the Anglican moral approach helps us to understand them.

It is frequently taught that 'attrition' is sorrow for sin through fear of punishment and 'contrition' is sorrow for sin for the love of God, whom it offends. While that is true, I think that there are two or three intermediate stages which are of practical value.

The first stage in growth is reached when, although we still very naturally fear punishment, we are nevertheless prepared to accept it. We have gained a clearer vision of the divine truth as it is expressed by God's justice, and this is the real meaning of the 'penance' given and accepted in sacramental confession. Some people say that this penance should be offered to God as a thanksgiving for grace and absolution. Perhaps that is permissible but I think it misses the point, for it fails to acknowledge the rightful punishment which is in accord with the divine justice. In the Middle Ages penances were very severe, which led to the opposite pastoral mistake: it tended to overrule divine mercy and implied that we could in some way atone for our own sin. Only our Lord's death and passion can do that, so it is right to see the penance as but a token acknowledgment, but I am led to wonder if our single psalm or collect does not go too far the other way. In normal practice we acknowledge our just deserts knowing full well that we are not going to get them.

But that is beside the point. It is much more important that we should learn to accept the crosses, misfortunes, and pains which the divine providence permits, not fatalistically but creatively as just and deserved. We must accept that, contrary to so much sentimentality aided by false psychology, punishment is not only just but one of the most completely human things there are. We are always hearing the view that criminals must be, not punished but reformed, because punishment is inhuman, degrading and contrary to our dignity; all of which is precisely what it is *not*. You reform a vicious horse or you train a puppy, but you can only punish a human being, which stresses rather than detracts from his status as a morally responsible and rational creature. I would prefer to be punished as a man rather than be treated like a motor that needed its plugs cleaned.

The Caroline moral approach helps again. The schoolboy who gets into mischief, who plays some prank, naturally tries not to be caught, but if he is caught he expects and accepts punishment, it is all part of the code. If in Christian context not to be caught implies inadvertent or ignorant sin, such an attitude is further proof of the absence of malice. It is the malicious youth who resents punishment because he is blinded to the meaning of justice—and probably of mercy as well: he is impenitent. The point which is missed is that if our young criminal is truly to be reformed, then the only healthy outcome of that reform

49

is penitence, proved by willingness to accept just punishment.

I do not wish to enter the lists of current penal controversy except to point out that a modicum of Christian psychology might clear up a good deal of sentimental misunderstanding. Strictly speaking there are no 'spiritual' and 'physical' sins because only the integrated and indivisible *man* commits sin, and if only the whole man sins it seems reasonable for the whole man to be punished. Moreover, imprisonment imprisons the whole man just as whipping punishes the whole man, so arguments about 'corporal' punishment, as such, are rather pointless. The modern attitude, and the whole position, is really summed up by the idea that no one must be 'humiliated.' If this means degraded as human beings then every one must agree, but if it means 'made humble' then that surely is the whole purpose. The stocks—nicely upholstered to comply with modern standards—have much to be said for them. The practical point is that we may accept 'physical' suffering like illness and discomfort as creative punishment, as purgation, as acknowledgment of divine justice, without harbouring the suspicion that God is rather out of date. We must face the Cross and stifle the schoolgirl cry that 'I am quite sure God would not wish that.'

The next stage of penitence is reached when we are prepared to accept suffering not only as just punishment for our own sins but vicariously, as our common share in the sins of the world and as the raw material of intercession : what might be called practical penitence. The thought of our Lord in his Passion and on the redemptive Cross shows that this kind of penitential intercession is the most Christlike activity we can achieve. It is what the Christian means by being 'outward looking,' not just 'carrying the Church into the world' by artificial stunts and propaganda, not simply 'being concerned about social problems'; but having a spiritual sensitivity and suppleness which grow from loyalty to the Church—necessary obedience—as the redemptive organism for the whole of creation. It is to look outward from the Church militant to God, taking in the whole world that comes within that vision. But first we must be *in* the Church: that is why our Offices, prayers and religious exercises are not insular piety but the foundation of it all, the daily pulse of the redemptive Body. Truly we should communicate and carry Christ into the world, it is still more important to lift the world into the Eucharistic oblation.

Now the *locus classicus* of impenitence is Exodus 7–12. Pharaoh saw the plagues of Egypt, not as the fruits of sin, not as blemishes on the good creation, not as just punishment, but as personal inconvenience. He was 'hard-hearted,' impenitent, narrow-minded, insensitive to truth, blind. Real penitence would have given him knowledge, a deeper vision of the truth, a practical wisdom. It would have made him 'soft-hearted' or, to use a better word, compassionate.

Towards the end of the last war most of us were 'hard-hearted,' we were accustomed to the horrors of aerial attack and unconcerned about the bombing of enemy cities: when two things happened. An atomic bomb devastated Hiroshima and we saw pictures of Belsen concentration camp. We were shocked and shaken, and I think we were moved to penitence and compassion. Like the plagues of Egypt these things were too big to ignore and the fact that one was caused by our allies and the other by the German Nazis made no difference. We sensed our solidity with the human race in a penitence and compassion which transcended national barriers. But we should not need such horrors to awaken our sensitivity towards the creation of God, all suffering and ugliness should stir us to penitence, and the more we progress, the nearer we get to the purple summit, the more compassionate we shall be. Such 'soft-heartedness' is no sentimental emotion, no swooning weakness, but the raw material of real intercession, which, in turn, is the mainspring of wise Christian action.

If Christ is to act upon our world through us, if we, the Church, are to be his true agents, his channel of redeeming grace, there can be no short cut. It remains useless to take a running jump at the mountain top: useless to undertake 'Christian' activity, be it social, political or evangelistic, that is dissociated from the sacraments of grace and the Offices of praise. There can be no creative religion without discipline and no redemption without suffering.

V

Sin and Creation

F o r particular self-examination, the capital sins form the only fool-proof system, comprising a deeply psychological and ascetical development of the decalogue, fully Christianized. For pastoral purposes the capital sins are sometimes said to be over-subtle and theoretical. Against the first charge I must counter that all other schemes, including the decalogue, are far too naïve for modern use, and that serious Christians need, and demand, something adult. It may be easier to answer the question 'Have I struck any one?' than to examine one's conscience in respect of 'anger,' but it is more satisfactory to make the initial effort to understand the meaning of anger than to plod through a list of twenty little questions which could come under this single head and still leave a good deal out. Let us remind ourselves once more than we are neither indulging a morbid interest in ourselves nor entering upon a juridical haggle. We are seeking the truth nurtured by penitence, we are facing the facts of life's practical data.

The second charge, that the capital sins are theoretical, without much relevance to everyday life, is unfortunately true in so far as they are frequently treated in just this way. We persist in thinking of a 'soul' isolated from its environment and in need of redemption, instead of seeing creation, including souls, in need of total redemption. We are taught what pride does to ourselves but not what it does to the town in which we live. Once this moral departmentalism is overcome, however, I think the capital sins cease to belong to medieval academics and become vitally relevant to twentieth century life. From this viewpoint, with special reference to the doctrine of creation, it is worth the effort to go through the list; not to overthrow the orthodox interpretation but to supplement it and perhaps to cast new light upon it.

Pride is the source of all other sin. It is usually defined as open rebellion against God, as preferring our own will to the divine will, as indulgent self-love against charity. All that is true, but left there it sounds remote from what everyday conscience knows as wrong-doing. Pride, the root-sin, is also the ultimate denial of the fact of creation, it is a refusal to accept the indisputable truth that we *are* creatures. It denies, or tries unsuccessfully to deny, that we and the whole creation are dependent on God from moment to moment, that all things are as they are because that is what God intends them to be. Margery Kempe, that exhilarating English fourteenth-century writer, calls herself 'this creature'; not as a term of self-abasement but of honour, as a plain statement of theological fact. On the other hand, Satan's sin consisted entirely in refusing this fact: he was an archangel but he was not prepared to admit it, he did not like being an archangel, he wanted to be God, so he wilfully rebelled against the whole order of creation. Those who do not like their bodies, who pretend they do not exist and try to pray like the angels, are not so malicious as Satan but they are making the same mistake.

According to the text-books, Pride, through the parent of all sin, begets three especially precocious offspring: presumption, ambition and vanity. If pride tries to contradict the *fact* of creation, the latter unholy trio try to upset its *order*. Pride makes men want to be angels, presumption makes good honest Christians want to be mystics.

Ambition is similar in that it makes us desire worldly position for which we are not intended, to seek honours and compliments which we do not deserve. It is like a policeman who creates chaos by leaving point duty because he thinks he ought to be a detective. It is presumption by which we refuse the humdrum discipline of prayers and Offices, of necessary obedience, because we think we ought to be contemplatives. This is not to support a rigid social *status quo*:

> God bless the squire and his relations
> And keep us in our proper stations—

because the opposite of ambition is contentment and humility, not apathy. There is nothing wrong with 'getting on' if God gives the talent and wants us to get on. But there is everything wrong with the rat-race because nobody ever wins.

Vanity is taking credit for what we are instead of giving it to the Creator; of all sins the most ludicrous it defies the first of all practical Christian rules: that we should not take ourselves too seriously.

In *Orthodoxy,* G. K. Chesterton puts forward the theory that our Lord went to the mountain-top, often to pray, but sometimes to have a quiet chuckle over the human world (Chap. 9). Rejecting the Apollinarian heresy and seeing Jesus as truly human, that theory seems to have a good deal to commend it. The glorious paradox we have to face is that human beings, with their ridiculous needs and habits, their absurd structure and shape, are thoroughly comic, yet God saw fit to become like unto them in all things and die for them on Calvary. That, to my mind, is the supreme and inviolable Christian apologetic because if the Incarnation is denied we are left either with scepticism or a bad joke. I sometimes wish that the vain, arrogant humanist would take a good look at himself in a full length mirror, preferably just after an attack of influenza. If human dignity exists at all it can only be by virtue of humility before the Incarnate Lord.

That is why the 'beatniks' are so admirably logical. To judge from what I saw of the genuine variety in Greenwich Village, the 'beatniks' are people who refuse to work, wash, shave, or do anything else. They cannot even be bothered to get into trouble. For rather different reasons, their attitude to money is not unlike that of St. Francis, and what little they get goes on drink and drugs. All this may well be a kind of passive protest against modern society. But if these brave people consciously reject the Incarnation, then they are acting with courage, conviction and logic, occasionally laced with a sense of humour. If we are not lifted up into Christ's sacred humanity, theirs is not only a reasonable but the consistent way to live. One must respect honest agnosticism, but 'respectable' agnosticism is a contradiction : human beings are too tragically comic for that.

Humility, the opposite of pride, is living in the truth. In Fr. Harton's words it is 'not feigning oneself to be less than one is but seeing oneself truly, as one is in the sight of God, nothing more nor less.' It is the joyful acceptance of creation, of the gifts and graces bestowed by God and a recognition of those which he has withheld. If a plain girl tries to make herself pretty she is vain, if a pretty girl says she is ugly she is telling a lie : neither has humility. If the first blames God for her plainness she is presumptuous, if the second thanks herself for her prettiness she is vain : both are guilty of pride. If both try to glorify God for what they are then they have attained to humility, if they rejoice in God for what they are, they have discovered the truth.

Envy follows when the plain girl is jealous of the pretty

one. It is to be envious of another's gifts, attributes or successes. This is another misinterpretation of creation which flows from an exaggerated individualism, and it shows up the dangers of a too narrow and too personal method of self-examination. For creation must be seen as an integrated design in which every one and everything has a part. Individual gifts and graces are given by God for particular purposes in the total plan, and they are withheld for the proper working of that same plan. Penitence becomes a search for the truth of one's own vocation. Envy inevitably causes disharmony in creation, society, and oneself, for it is to throw spanners into the works of divine Providence. Diabolically, envy, which starts with intense individualism, ends by destroying individuality. In modern society its end product is a sheepish following of fashion, of 'keeping up with the Joneses.' We accept neither our deficiencies nor our gifts when we envy those of others; which makes modern society like a football team of eleven goalkeepers.

Within the life of the Church, especially the local Church, we are led back to the doctrine of diverse gifts within the unity of the Body, to the dependence of the mystic upon the humdrum discipline of ordinary Christians, and of our real share in the glory of the saints, however far from sanctity we are. It is still a matter of 'necessary obedience.'

Among other things, some obvious and others less so, *anger* contradicts the 'first form of contemplation,' of being in harmony with the created world, of being 'at home' with people and environment. Here it is especially important not to dissociate morals from ascetic, for anger is essentially a distraction, because it interferes with recollection of God in creation. Jesus taught that if a man steals your coat you are not to prosecute but give him your cloke as well (Matthew 5 : 40). St. Paul told the Corinthians not to bother with lawsuits but rather to be defrauded (1 Cor. 6 : 1–8). Now it seems to me that in terms of pure ethics, this teaching makes no sense at all, in fact if we left the matter there the result would be chaos. But I do not think that our Lord and St. Paul had no respect for ordinary human rights, nor do I find much satisfaction in the evasive theory that this is 'idealistic' ethic. I prefer to think that it is ascetical-ethic. Coats and clokes are good and important things, human rights in society matter very much, but they do not matter as much as habitual recollection; it is not worth bothering about clothes if it hinders your relation with God. You cannot be in harmony with creation, you cannot rejoice in it, you cannot say your prayers and praise God if you are in a furious temper. There may be righteous indignation but that is concerned with detraction from the glory of God, not with coats and clokes. Any other sort of anger is a waste of spiritual energy, it may be justified, it may be excusable, but we are concerned with facts not fine points of the law : if you want to get to the top of the mountain it is best to avoid fighting on the way up.

In this context, *covetousness* is not quite so simple as it looks. The text-books define it as the 'inordinate love of worldly goods' which is correct but misleading, for there is a sense in which St. Francis, the least covetous of men, loved worldly goods more than any one. Covetousness is rather a lack of love for creatures, thence an inordinate desire to own, exploit and abuse them. It is materialism, the failure to understand that creatures are to glorify God in their own particular way and to help us to do the same.

I must now be bold enough to accuse some of the text-books of more serious ambiguity. Worldly goods are often divided into those which are *necessary* to human life, those which are *useful,* and *luxuries.* The *impression* we get, even if it is not bluntly stated, is that the first are good, the second tolerable and the third group positively bad; which seems to me to be a very materialistic, if not impious, way of looking at things. The plain truth is that because of human frailty, a sophisticated society, false values, ambition, 'status symbols,' and that sort of nonsense, luxuries can so easily lead to real covetousness, they can be 'occasions of sin,' but then so can a good many other things. The text-books are right in warning that 'luxurious living' is not very conducive to spiritual progress, and that it is sometimes difficult to gaze at a new, shiny, expensive motor-car without the fleeting idea that it would be nice to have one, probably for all sorts of dubious motives.

I do not think any of the three saints of creation we thought about in chapter III would refuse a Rolls Royce if they were offered one. Hugh of St. Victor would see it as the rich fruit of meditation on the symbolic universe, which had led men to a greater understanding of it. He would see it as his kind of science which is almost indistinguishable from religion. I think St. Francis would accept it if it were given him as alms although I am a little doubtful if he would keep it very long. But St. Thomas would revel in it and love it because it perfectly fulfilled the purpose for which it was made.

In short, whatever the dangers of our frailty and concupiscence, we cannot and dare not call caviare, Napoleon brandy, Savile Row suits and diamond rings, *bad,* because they are all very obviously *good.* We overcome covetousness, not by turning our backs on creation but by trying to admire and understand it more perfectly, not by hating things but by loving them more truly.

The Purple Headed Mountain

There is a little story of a medieval friar who ministered to a group of isolated villages. He had to walk many miles each day from one to another until a kind parishioner gave him a very beautiful donkey to ride on, and being a good Franciscan he accepted it with some misgivings. He tied it up outside the first village church and said Mass amidst a great deal of distraction. He could not be recollected for worrying about the donkey so he untied it and drove it away with a friendly whack; he was not going to let a donkey interfere with his devotion. Having trudged to the next village, and arrived late, he found the donkey quietly waiting for him at the church door, so he said Mass with great devotion and no anxiety at all; and rode happily away on the donkey. The moral of the story, of course, is that it had to be an exceptionally good donkey, clever, strong, good tempered, well trained, and therefore very valuable: it had to be a luxury donkey, a Rolls Royce donkey. Nothing less would have done.

Gluttony is a particular form of covetousness, the misuse of, and lack of respect for, that particular group of creatures which God supplies for our sustenance. Eating and drinking are minor pleasures of life and I do not think God made them pleasurable by accident. I think he meant it. *Lust* is similarly the misuse of, and in an obviously special sense the lack of reverence for, the whole process of creation. And if pride is essentially the failure to accept the fact of creation, *sloth* is the refusal to accept its glorious implications. Pride looks at creation and fails to understand it, sloth looks at creation and turns away.

I hope I have not given the impression that, because all creatures are good, there is no need to curb our tastes and desires. That would be plain nonsense, but we should try to remember that discipline is needed because we are con-

cupiscent not because creatures are bad, and that our ultimate aim is to reach God on the mountain top and sometimes good creatures can hinder the climb. We should
recognize that our scale of values is hopelessly twisted and
artificial. Every one is aware that if kippers were thirty
shillings each and oysters ten a penny, then the kitchens of
the wealthy would reek of kippers three times a week. The
sensible Christian, acknowledging his stewardship and the
needs of others, forgoes the oysters and eats kippers, but
he does not put up with them, he revels in his thankful
enjoyment of them.

The traditional discipline which helps us to keep things
in perspective is fasting, and I daresay some of my more
conventional readers have been tearing their hair for some
time : here we are, three-quarters of the way through a
'Lent book' and fasting has only just been mentioned ! But
I am not ashamed and I do not think that I am putting it
far from its proper place. Fasting is a sensible discipline,
but something is a little misplaced when devout Christians
are horrified by meat on Friday and feel no responsibility
at all for the daily Office of praise. It is only common sense
for a football team to refrain from suet pudding just before
a match, but there is little point in it for those who do not
play the game itself. I know one particularly dreadful list
of self-examination questions—published in 1901—which
contains : 'Have you made your communion *every month* :
WERE YOU FASTING ?' The italics are mine but the capitals
are not ! Much as I favour fasting communion, this surely
earns first prize for putting the cart before the horse.

The clue to the matter is this : in the seventeenth chapter
of St. Matthew's gospel, when the disciples had been singularly ineffective in their exercise of spiritual power over
evil, our Lord rebuked them for faithlessness, but faith is

nurtured by prayer: 'howbeit this kind goeth not out but by prayer.' The scholars say that that is the original ending of verse 21, but that later some scribe or editor saw fit to add 'and fasting.' That gets things in the right order, fasting is an indispensable aid to prayer but it has little value in itself. The human spirit is like a powerful horse which nevertheless achieves little without training and harnessing. If prayer without discipline is as a horse without harness, fasting without prayer is like harness without a horse: which is singularly useless. How, then, should we fast intelligently, in Lent or at any other time? Among others, I suggest that there are four main ways.

First, as an aid to recollection. This is the ordinary Friday fast used as an act of recollection of our Lord's most precious death. Thus any minor Lenten abstention is meant to help us enter into a living fellowship with Christ in the wilderness. These, generally, are the types of fasts laid down by the Church.

Secondly, as an indirect aid to prayer. That is to help eradicate sinful tendencies and besetting sins, and generally to control mind and will *in order that* our prayer and worship can grow.

Thirdly, as a direct aid to prayer, like the pre-communion fast or, for that matter, the immediate preparation for any prayer: we cannot make meditations when we are full up with treacle pudding. More especially there are fasts in terms of time, fasts from pleasures, which make time for prayer: a very little less sleep, a little less time with novel, radio or newspaper, and the daily Office would offer no difficulty at all. That, to my mind, would be far more valuable than a lot of subjective little devotions, and more creative than many disciplines of greater austerity.

Fourthly, let us always try to fast in the Franciscan

spirit; not because creatures are bad but because they are so supremely good that they are worth offering up to God with tremendous reverence. 'Stewardship' means that we are guests in God's world, we are here to make use of his creatures not by right but by his invitation. You can refuse hospitality or make too free with it, and it is difficult to decide which is the more insulting to your host. As Chesterton says, we can give God thanks for beer and burgundy by not drinking too much of them (*Orthodoxy,* Chap. 9).

VI

Meditation: Christ and Creation

WHEN I suggested that to meet modern contingencies it might be wise for laypeople to use the daily Office without the lessons, I was careful to add that this did *not* mean that regular use of the Scriptures was unimportant. Later we concluded that meditation upon the person of Jesus was the best way to achieve penitence, the firmest basis for self-examination, and the source of moral theology; in short that it trained the conscience. The 'schoolgirl conscience' is quite sure that Jesus would never behave violently in church, and that he is always gentle with natural things. Meditation on the cleansing of the temple and the cursing of the barren fig tree forces us to modify this subjective and sentimental idea; our religious outlook becomes more mature.

Anglicans who make meditations according to some form of the 'three point' method, the disciplined consideration of the Gospel story by imagination, intellect and will, confront four main difficulties; or so it would appear from my own pastoral experience. It might be useful, and it is certainly consonant to our general themes, to try to help with these difficulties.

The first is a sense of unrealness due, I am certain, to veiled Apollinarianism: the failure to face our Lord's complete humanity. We all gladly acknowledge the wonderful truth whenever we say the creeds, especially when we say the *Quicunque vult,* and I am sure that all serious Church people firmly believe it. But this dogma is not carried over into mental prayer; because of an understandable but nevertheless false sense of devotion we jib at attributing human physical functions and processes to the Son of God. To be very blunt—which is seldom bad pastoral practice— we do not like the idea of Jesus Christ digesting food with teeth, tongue and stomach, we do not like acknowledging his real hunger and thirst, his human fear and anger, his sexual and aesthetic emotions, his loneliness and pain. I repeat that this is understandable, but I must also repeat that it is absolutely wrong. We must try to realize that even now, after the Ascension, Jesus is still and will ever remain, fully and completely Man, as truly human as we one day hope to be when we are perfected and glorified in heaven. Unless we carry over this doctrine into our meditations our Lord appears but a vague and shadowy idea. We must struggle to see him as he is : 'God, of the substance of the Father, begotten before the worlds : and Man, of the substance of his mother, born in the world ; Perfect God, and perfect man : of a reasonable soul and human flesh subsisting.' That passage from the *Quicunque vult* contains two phrases which are especially important if we are to overcome this difficulty. First, 'of the substance of his mother.' Far from 'interfering with our devotion to Christ' as some would put it, constant recognition of, and devotion to, the Blessed Mother safeguards the true humanity of the divine Son. Secondly, 'born in the world.' It is impossible to perceive full humanity except in a fully human environment. To use the technical terms, we do not take enough care over 'composition of place,' the initial process of setting the scene of our meditation, of seeing Jesus in particular places, and considering his relations to things, creatures, creation.

This is the second main difficulty. As it is perhaps natural to think of our Lord's divinity at the expense of his humanity, so it is also natural to concentrate on the person of Christ rather than his surroundings: despite Apollinarian tendencies, we have some idea of our Lord's appearance, but do we know what the room at Cana was really like? how big was the cursed fig tree? what sort of a place was the wilderness? We have probably not tried very hard to find out. But that is a mistake because Christ will not be a living man to us unless he is living and acting somewhere in an environment. The proper technique is vividly taught in the *Book of Margery Kempe*. In her meditations, Jesus might be in first century Palestine or fourteenth century Norfolk, but he is always in some vigorously living place, and he is seldom alone, he is surrounded by the disciples or the holy women, and therefore he is vividly alive and human.

The third difficulty about meditation is that people will approach the Bible with an unnatural tension: it is 're-ligion' in the wrong sense, something isolated from life. Yet the art of meditation is very much the same as the art of reading history, or even a novel: characters will not live unless we give our imagination free rein, nor will they live unless we have the scenes firmly held in the mind. The country house where the crime was committed, the little town where the spies are in hiding, the school where the detective is masquerading as a master: all these are as clear as can be, but the home at Nazareth, the town of Bethany, the Mount of Olives, what are they like? Few of the faithful have any idea because all this is 'in the Bible' so we must be serious, tense, mock-devout and half asleep while we read it: but in heaven's name *why?*

To overcome this attitude, there are three hints which I, and I think others, have found useful. It is sometimes held to be a good thing to make meditations kneeling in church, but that it is *permissible* to meditate anywhere. I would put it the other way round, and I would go so far as to recommend an arm-chair by a quiet fireside as the best possible circumstances for the exercise : I doubt if the most brilliant novel would really live if you read it kneeling in church. This is one reason why I am doubtful if the middle of the Church's Office is the best place for long and elaborate Scriptural lessons.

Another difficulty is the idea that one should always meditate according to some rigid plan. On occasion, perhaps during Lent, there is much to be said for working steadily through one of the Gospels, but there is nothing sacrosanct about such plans. I think that there are at least two other ways : our Lord's life and teaching covers every human contingency, whatever our present problem or interest, there is a parable, saying or incident which is relevant to it, and which could throw light upon it. That, now, to-day, seems the sensible meditation to make. And it is sometimes very illuminating to meditate on groups of stories : Jesus refused to turn stones into bread, he refused drugged wine on the Cross, he changed water into wine at Cana. The three stories together give a fuller knowledge of our Lord than any of them separately.

The last hint is that some of the text-books say that meditation concludes with a definite *resolution*. Sometimes it does but I think this can be exaggerated. The primary purpose is to know our Lord, to try to understand his mind, and to grow nearer to him in love. Constant meditation inevitably tends towards that end against which the absence of particular resolutions is comparatively unimportant.

The fourth general difficulty is inherent in the phrase 'meditation and Bible study,' which is wont to be used rather loosely. The fact of the matter is that these two exercises are completely different. Both are necessary within the Church, both may be used by the individual Christian, but they must not be confused. 'Bible study' rightly implies a careful study of the Scriptures to discover, or substantiate, the doctrine of the Church, and it demands a rigid intellectual discipline. Meditation, on the other hand, is an attempt to meet the living Christ, almost to take him out of the Bible and place him in contemporary circumstances and society. It consequently allows, or even demands, a much greater imaginative freedom. The confusion between the two leads to an uncreative tension; we are so afraid of misinterpreting 'what the Bible means' that we find ourselves in a spiritual strait-jacket. I have suggested elsewhere that if the proper end of Biblical scholarship is Christian doctrine, the proper end of meditation is Christian art, or even the Biblical novel; and of course the fruits as well as the techniques must never be confused. It would be silly for a scholar to criticize Giotto because the details of his paintings are unbiblical. It would be equally wrong for a novelist like Sholem Asch or Lloyd Douglas to claim that their books were Christian doctrine.

When I am on a long journey I sometimes like to think of our Lord sitting in the car beside me. That is a sensible act of recollection, and it is no use the scholars objecting because there is no record of Jesus riding in a car. It would be equally wrong for me to claim that he did and start building theories on it. But of course meditation is necessarily guided by grace and so the plain fact is this: complete imaginative freedom in meditation is earned by 'necessary obedience,' so let us make our Communion regularly, recite the Office constantly, live truly with the mystical Body; then sit in an arm-chair with the New Testament and give our imaginative faculties reasonable freedom : let our Lord really live in our hearts and in our homes. But we are in danger so soon as any vital part of the *total* Christian life gets left out.

It will have been noticed that all these difficulties arise, to a greater or lesser extent, through the failure to give full weight to the doctrine of creation : Apollinarianism, inadequate 'composition of place,' tenseness deriving from an over 'religious' attitude to the Bible. And it is particularly important to overcome these errors if our meditations are to help with the three things in which we are particularly interested : mature self-examination of conscience, creative penitence, and an understanding of moral theology. To give but one pastoral example, people frequently confuse temptation, or even normal human awareness, with 'sins of thought.' The normal thoughts and reactions of men confronted with creatures, with food, drink, women, 'luxuries,' are regarded as suspect long before there is temptation, let alone sin. This is because creatures are themselves suspect and none of these thoughts and reactions are seen to apply to our Lord's own consciousness : he is not *really* man. The result is a 'schoolgirl conscience.'

What may not have been noticed is that if we meditate on our Lord's attitude towards, and use of, created things, we find support for the theories of the three saints of creation we have already considered. Or, to put it the better way round, we discover that their ascetical theology, far from being abstract, theoretical and artificial, is thoroughly Biblical. It has been worked out not by academic thinking but by constant meditation on Christ in creation. This particular ascetic theology could easily develop into a vast book in itself. It must suffice to give one or two examples.

Our Lord's attitude to the creation was that of St. Francis : he loved all things and possessed nothing. He wholeheartedly loved the sparrows and the lilies as children of the Father, but they were also symbols, and he saw, with St. Hugh of St. Victor, that their existence meant something; it taught that if God looked after them in love, so men and women could rely on the divine Providence. But the Victorines failed to see the further point: you must not take this symbolism too literally because—and here against St. Francis—sparrows and lilies are less than men: 'Ye are more value than many sparrows,' 'How much more will he clothe you' (Matthew 6: 26–32). That, as we have seen, is 'Thomism.' Jesus recognizes the signs, symbols, of harvest and of the weather, and teaches on the signs of the end (Mark 13: 4–8, 24). His parables are symbolic teaching which has not to be interpreted too literally, they are 'earthly stories with a heavenly meaning,' and that is no bad substitute for the more pompous Thomist phrase 'analogical discontinuity.' The Star of the Nativity and the Dove of the Baptism are Victorine symbols, but there is always the warning against too literal, too logical, sign-seeking, there can be no mere wonders, no too obvious sign of Christ's divinity: the Jews were refused those because religion must advance by jumps of faith, not by demonstration but by analogy (Matthew 12: 38–40; 16, 1–4).

The miracles too are subtle signs of the divine power, they are to teach, not merely astound. The storm is stilled and the forces of gravity overruled because creation is a continuous process of love, not a system of infallible laws, and the Creator incarnate in Christ has the right to change the process as the artist, and only the artist, has the right to alter his own picture: prayer controls matter. Our Lord heals disease, blindness, lameness and paralysis, he cures mental disorder like that of the Gadarine maniac, yet the healing is always 'spiritual' in the full sense: it applies always to the whole, integrated man—'Thy sins are for-given thee, *therefore*, walk' (Mark 2 : 10, 11).

Christ furiously throws doves, tables and coins out of the temple, not because they are bad but because they are in the wrong place at the wrong time for the wrong reason. He curses the barren fig tree and it withers away ('I'm sure God would never do a thing like that!') probably as a subtle sign against uncreative Pharisaism, but also for the best of all Thomist principles : it was not fulfilling the pur-pose for which it was created, it bore no fruit to the glory of God, it rejected its 'spiritual gifts.'

That is very cursory, but I think it is the sort of medita-tion that is well worth making : simply to ask ourselves, as we look at the whole gospel, 'What was Jesus' attitude to, and use of, all the creatures which make up his necessary environment?'

For the rest of the book, let us look at parts of the New Testament in the same meditative mood, to see if it can illustrate and enlighten some of the points already discussed.

VII

The Temptation

LENT is the Church's re-enactment of Christ's forty days in the wilderness; an episode of inexhaustible depth and subtlety. It is no wonder that sermons and addresses on the Temptation are so diverse, each emphasizing a particular aspect of it. But I think it is a pity that so often there is a suggestion of undue passivity on our Lord's part. We are given the impression that Jesus found himself in the wilderness for no apparent reason, that he fasted for no particular purpose, when the devil, cleverly lying in ambush, swooped down to tempt him. Then it is implied that, in spite of this unfortunate situation, in spite of weakness and hunger, Jesus just managed to resist. It is the fight against heavy odds, the backs to the wall stand so loved by English military historians, and it contains an element of truth. But there is another side.

'Then was Jesus led up of the Spirit into the wilderness, to be tempted of the devil' (Luke 4 : 1). That plain statement—and there appear to be no special subtleties in translation—suggests that the boot might have been on the other foot. If Jesus is God and the Spirit is God it means that Jesus made a free, clear-cut decision to go into the wilderness for a very definite purpose. Victory over demonic powers goeth not out but by prayer, and, as useful support to prayer, fasting. So Christ fasted, again for a very definite reason : forty days of prayer, aided by a fast, was a carefully planned preparation for war, it was a systematic ascetical campaign, a well constructed Rule, not to make our Lord weak but to make him strong. Then Satan 'came to him'; he had to, he had been sought out and caught in a well laid trap. Christ declared war and held the initiative all the time, which in no way diminishes the reality and bitterness of the struggle. Jesus Christ came to save the world; this initial conquest was part of the plan, it was no fortuitous occurrence but a major battle in a cosmic campaign.

If we may look at it in this way, the Temptation story throws light upon some of the practical pastoral questions we have been considering. Let us look, not at an Apollinarian symbol floating about in a vacuum, but at the Son of God in a particular place. The wilderness is not an abstract negation but a positive part of creation. Perhaps it was the ideal terrain for this battle or perhaps it was chosen as the infertile symbol of sin now to be defeated: 'the whole creation groaneth and travaileth in pain,' but 'the wilderness shall be glad, the desert shall rejoice, and blossom as the rose.'

Most people prefer Switzerland to the Sahara, the Cotswolds to the Fens; the former are more inspiring, more awesome, more plainly a manifestation of the mind of God as we prefer to imagine it. But in spite of the Pauline theory just quoted, I do not think the desert is desert, entirely because of sin, or because God got bored and allowed the rivers to dry up: it is there for a purpose. The barren wastes are necessary when our spiritual energy needs conserving without distraction. Hugh of St. Victor might have seen rivers, valleys and forests as symbols of spiritual consolation, as edifying, even as glorious liturgy, and the wilderness, or the farming of the Fens, as the necessary obedience of plodding spiritual stamina, of the humdrum daily discipline. William of St. Thierry might be eager to point out that, compared with the lakes and wooded hills, the flat dreary fen was a good deal more productive. It is wonderful to worship in York Minster, but if we cannot find God and fight Satan in a tin shed we are still in the spiritual kindergarten.

The wilderness has become a symbol for a quiet place of prayer or retreat; the church in a city backwater, the remote country church or retreat house. But the emphasis is still in danger of being one-sided unless we use both interpretations of our Lord's Temptation. Retreat and prayer are too often thought of as 'being quiet with God,' as a kind of holy rest cure, as something calm, gentle and consoling. That attitude is not wrong, but it is only half the story. To enter a quiet place, to go into retreat, is also to seek out Satan—on our own initiative—and attack. To kneel down in prayer is also to stand up and fight, for although we must resist temptation throughout the busy day, it is in the wilderness that the real battle is won or lost. One cannot 'lead a good life' without prayers, sacraments and Rule any more than battles can be won without training, arms and strategy.

Some people regard the Religious Orders, especially contemplative Orders, as 'withdrawn from the world' selfishly and irresponsibly. On the contrary they form the real front line of the battle for world redemption, for they are imitating the Lord's Lenten activity in the wilderness: which was neither selfish nor irresponsible. The devil and his demons are the ultimate source of all sin and misery, and by God's grace we may occasionally deliver a telling blow or two against them, knowing all too well that we are bound to be hit back sooner or later. Only in the contemplative cloister is the devil perpetually groggy and it is strengthening to realize that the Church is one, the battle is one. When our personal sector looks a little shaky we know that further along the line the demonic armies are in flight. To be envious of the contemplative and mystic, to be discouraged by our comparison with the saints, is as silly as if a platoon in retreat was annoyed because the rest of the regiment was conquering.

Let us, however, consider one part of our own fight which is victorious. The confessional is the most deserted place in the world, a wilderness more remote than the Sahara. We enter it through penitence, the purposeful driving force, and, being Anglicans, we go there on our own initiative, not to pick fine legal points but to make a full and generous self-oblation at the foot of the victorious Cross. But fully to surrender to Jesus Christ is total onslaught upon the devil; meekly to yield to Christ is to charge, and here if nowhere else we have Satan just exactly where we want him : cornered, battered and cringing. This is one round we must win because Christ has won it for us, in the wilderness; our weapon is Christ, our arms are Christ, our power is Christ. However wounded when we enter, here we must win. In the confessional we deliver the knock-out blow, and I am sufficiently anti-Apollinarian to believe that our Blessed Lord will not only absolve but applaud.

The devil is real, and I think we usually make one of two mistakes about him. Either we deny his existence or we give him more dignity than he deserves. The former error is fatal, and we should realize that in the cosmic, Biblical sense, he is no myth or fiction but an historical character, the fallen archangel. To deny the existence of angels, archangels and the host of heaven is to a deny a large part of the doctrine of creation; it is to deny St. Thomas' hierarchy of being from inanimate matter to God, for to omit the realm of pure spirit is to take a very narrow view of creation. It is like the tourist who spends a fortnight in Park Lane and thinks that he has seen England. If there are angels, upon which the Church insists, and if there is evil, which there too obviously is, then there must be demons. The characteristic work of demons is disorder, in body, mind and spirit, in civilization and society; the characteristic of hell is chaos, the opposite of creation : a land without order as the book of Job describes it. All this conflict is what St. Augustine calls concupiscence, and whatever our increased knowledge of how its fruits develop, in mental disease and so on, we cannot explain why it occurs without reference to the fallen Archangel.

The other mistake is less serious but it is worth recognizing. In the profound theology of G. K. Chesterton, the devil fell through taking himself too seriously, since there is nothing so ridiculous as a creature trying to be God. The devil is dangerous but he is also grotesque. While properly estimating the fury of the battle, we must subject Satan to the scorn and ridicule he deserves, and we must constantly employ the weapons he fears : prayer and fasting; humility, penitence and truth; confession, grace, spiritual discipline; Rule which is order.

In the wilderness Christ refused to turn stones into bread, on the Cross he refused wine, at Cana he miraculously created 120 gallons of it. Jesus never did things in moderation, he always did them generously and perfectly. These three episodes together throw a good deal of light on ascetical theory. Apart from more subtle reasons, the spiritual struggle in the wilderness demanded a continuation of the fast which supported prayer. Our Saviour had to make the final oblation of himself on the Cross with perfect obedience of mind and will, drugs would have interfered with it. He refused nothing at Cana, not I think because he was relaxing, because there was no great job on hand, but because this too was all part of a truly human ascetical plan. As I have said before, truly to keep, to observe, the Church's joyous festivals is as much a part of total Christian life as observing its penitential fasts. First things must come first, there must be order, but all the time, stones, bread, water, drugs, wine, remain very good parts of a very good creation.

I am aware that the story of the Cana marriage has given the scholars all sorts of headaches, many doubt its authenticity, and I am in no position to argue with them. But do we miss the point that it was *good* wine, much too good for those who were 'well drunken,' and that Jesus was not defying his principles by making blatant signs of his Godhead but that he was human enough to give an embarrassed host an acceptable present? I further suspect that there are some who object to the story because 'they are quite sure that God would never do a thing like that.'

VIII

Gethsemane

THE agony in the Garden of Gethsemane is the climax of a group of stories in which our Lord's prayer follows a clear pattern, an ascetical progress through four stages. The same pattern is found, for example, in the stories of the raising of Lazarus and of the expulsion of Judas Iscariot from the Upper Room. All these are worth a great deal of meditation, and here I shall be content just to suggest the plan underlying these prayers, and to add six pastoral points arising out of it.

First, all these stories begin with our Lord being 'troubled in spirit' as a result of an event or situation of a very practical kind. He foresees treachery by a chosen disciple, he is compassionate in the human sorrow of Mary and Martha, perhaps angry with the hypocrisy of the wailing Jews, and possibly worried by the faithlessness of them all. Secondly, he takes the problem to the Father in absolutely honest prayer, he bluntly argues the thing out with God without any semblance of mock-piety. In Gethsemane he plainly requests that 'this cup be taken from him'—'Father save me from this hour.' As Friedrich Heiler points out so well in *Prayer,* Jesus has a perfectly normal human fear of pain and death, and he repeats a plea for deliverance three times before he is convinced that the Passion is his duty and the Father's will. At Bethany he twice 'groaned in spirit' before he knew how to act. Thirdly, only after this kind of long, agonizing struggle, this fierce argument with God in colloquy, is it possible even for the Incarnate Son perfectly to surrender to the divine will. The consummation of the prayer, and the fourth stage, is an outpouring of adoring love : 'Father glorify thy name,' in the Upper Room 'now is the Son of man glorified, and God is glorified in him.' At Bethany it is 'said I not unto thee, that, if thou wouldest believe, thou shouldest see the glory of God. . . . Father I thank thee that thou hast heard me.' So we have 1. 'troubling in spirit' ; 2. long, honest, earnest colloquy ; 3. surrender ; 4. adoration. These are the six points which follow from this total spiritual experience.

1. Our 'spiritual' life is our complete life. We assemble in churches for common worship, we retire to the quiet of the wilderness for prayer, but it all begins with, and cannot be dissociated from, the world of creatures and circumstances. The Church which is true to itself *is* in the world, it does not have to *go* there. Christianity *is* life, they do not have to be artificially glued together. Worry is sinful, but 'to be troubled' is to be sensitive and compassionate, and for us the acquiring of these virtues demands penitence. Compassion in the world is the raw material of intercession. It is what the Church really means by 'looking outward,' and it is the secret of its true influence, of redemption, evangelism and witness.

2. Our petition and intercession must be *honest*. If what we feel to be God's will is unpleasant, then go and tell him ; if we are anxious then go to God and discuss the matter ; if our prayers and Offices are burdensome, our worship dull and our communion empty, then go to God and say so : then listen. That is precisely what Jesus did in Gethsemane, and he had to argue and struggle and sweat blood before he could finally say 'Thy will be done.' Prayer does not consist of strings of mock-pious phrases and sentimental

clichés, nor of other people's compositions offered out of a book second-hand at certain times. There is a lot to be said for the devout old Irish woman who was wont to command her numerous family : 'Well don't just sit there, *pray* something.'

3. Only after this sort of struggle is 'surrender' possible, and surrender issues in peace and knowledge of God's design. So surrender, 'abandonment to the divine Providence,' is quite the reverse of fatalism, stoicism or determinism, the idea that 'what will be, will be.' Surrender to God is not passivity but an active exercise of will : to yield to Christ is to attack the devil and all his works.

4. In the face of all this how childish, even blasphemous, it is to be worried if our prayer is not always comfortable and consoling, to think of our faith as something gentle and helpful, a nice stand-by when we happen to feel like it. Here too is the answer to those who want prayer to be 'simple' and not cluttered up with methods, systems and techniques. Our Lord's prayer, in Gethsemane, Bethany and in the Upper Room, was anything but simple. It was very complicated but it was also orderly, for here is what later asceticists would call a 'four-fold progression.' Some of the jargon grew up with the newer needs of the Middle Ages ; it continues to evolve to meet the intellectual needs of the present day, but the Church's plans, methods, systems, and all the rest are firmly based on the New Testament, and in this case on our Lord's own experience.

5. We must have courage to face up to doubts, distractions, and difficulties. There is a movement in the Church of England to make everything 'easily understood by the average congregation.' In one sense that is sensible, there is no point in making difficulties, but if the policy were to

eliminate all the mysteries, there would not be much of the Faith left. In the Baptism service, for example, the statement that we are 'born in sin' is open to misunderstanding, it also offends fond parents and Godparents, but it happens to be true. In 1928 the phrase was changed to 'prone to sin,' which sounds much nicer, but it has the rather serious objection of being, to my mind, blatant heresy. Or again, it will be readily admitted that a few parts of the Psalter express some curious sentiments for the praise of God. Psalm 58 does not sound much like a hymn of adoration, so the revisers of 1928 said we could omit it. (I always feel that the prim little brackets round the fierce verses would have delighted the heart of Thomas Bowdler.) But then Gethsemane is a curious sort of colloquy between the Father and the Son. The Cross hardly struck every one as the obvious way of redeeming the world. The answer to these mysteries, for the 'average congregation' or any one else, cannot be found by running away from them. It is, of course, the same old 'schoolgirl conscience'—'I am quite sure God would not like that.'

6. Finally, although the safe test for spiritual progress is moral theology, that there is growth in spirit when we commit fewer sins, irrespective of feelings, results or anything else, there is a sound test here for individual prayers. They are good prayers, good meditations, when they naturally conclude with praise, with spontaneous acts of adoration : 'Father glorify thy name.' For this is the proper end of all prayer, irrespective of affective experience or resolutions. And Gethsemane and the Cross underline that constant mystery : how creative and acceptable our periods of aridity and desolation can be.

F

IX

Magdalene

ONE of the most practical doctrines of the very practical theology of St. Thomas Aquinas is that 'grace perfects nature.' Every one is created by God with a unique character which is spoiled by sin and restored by grace. Life in the Church, life 'in grace,' is a continuous process of redemption, the climb up the mountain, the progress towards an end. The important thing, which is always being overlooked by Christians who make great efforts in their faith, is that our unique nature, as God has created it, is to be redeemed, perfected, glorified, but it is not to be repressed, stunted or changed into something else. Sometimes it is difficult to distinguish between our innate characteristics, the essential parts of our nature, and secondary characteristics acquired by habit or environment, and we usually need a spiritual guide to help sort things out. But having thought seriously about that, our job is to try, by the aid of grace, to perfect ourselves as we are, and not to ape others or conform to a type or try to change into something different.

'Conversion' may be defined as a 'change of heart,' or a 'change of outlook,' which is true if it means a turning from the deceitful pleasures of sin to truthful joy in Christ, but it must not mean changing into a different kind of person altogether, and Christians will persist in trying to do just that. In defiance of the doctrine of creation, we fall for the terrible idea that the 'Christian character' implies a uniform mediocrity. We submit to the tenet of 'moderation in all things,' so loved by Victorian schoolmasters, which is about as unChristian as any idea could be : we are not called to be moderate, we are called to be perfect. You have only to look at any of the saints to see how wrong that attitude is : whatever they were, Peter, Augustine, Bernard, Francis, Teresa, can scarcely be called moderate or inhibited. And God clearly chose Paul because he wanted to sanctify and use the religious courage, insight and integrity which were always inherent in Saul. So it is with any of the 'twice-born' saints.

In practice, an arrogant extrovert must try, under the influence of grace, to become a humble extrovert, but he should not try to be a humble introvert. A beautiful woman must beware of vanity, but she would sin gravely if she mutilated herself, and I think she would risk a sort of perverted vanity if she went out of her way to look dowdy. If meditation is our normal way of prayer we must try to make a better meditation to-day than we did yesterday, and a better one still to-morrow, but we should not try to be contemplatives, unless or until God makes it clear that that is what he intends us to be. When Dr. Albert Schweitzer left the intellectual society of Europe for the African jungle he insisted that he was making no 'renunciation' of himself or his great talents, but that he was perfecting himself and consecrating his talents in a way that he thought God intended (*My Life and Thought*, chap. 9).

But I should say that the most perfect example of this doctrine in action—'grace perfects nature'—is to be found in the story of St. Mary Magdalene. There is not much historical evidence for her early life, but a very strong tradition, enlightened by the New Testament, leaves little doubt as to the kind of woman she was : a common harlot 'out of whom went seven devils' (Luke 8 : 2), all the

F*

capital sins churned up into a vile mixture. I imagine her as impetuous, generous according to her lights, extravagant, sensuous, alluring and over-sexed. I see her parading about in powder and paint, wearing exotic clothes and perfume. Now some of the devotional books give much the same picture, and go on to say that she was converted and changed completely. The glorious thing is that she was converted and did not change at all; she changed her way of living but she never changed herself, she never turned into a different woman. Her innate characteristics, which had led her into a slough of sin, became sanctified and perfected, through grace, penitence, and love.

She remained a woman of impetuous, generous, full-blooded love, she had to express herself physically, through her senses, she could never be content with the sort of 'spiritual' religion which pretended she had no body and no passion. Once she kissed and caressed her revolting clients; now she kissed and caressed the feet of Christ, pouring tears of penitence upon them and wiping them lovingly, not with a towel but with her hair, with a physical part of herself (Luke 7 : 36–9). And our Lord let her, sternly ordering the objectors to leave her alone. On the Resurrection morning he forbade her to touch him, but for reasons which I take to be more metaphysical than moral.

I have never been able to find out exactly what ointment of spikenard is (Mark 14 : 3). All the New Testament tells us is that Mary anointed our Lord with it as a symbolic embalming, prophetic of his death, and that it was very expensive. It was probably some kind of cosmetic, perhaps the first century counterpart to the sort of preparation now produced by Messieurs Chanel and Picot. If that is a fair guess, is it too much to suggest that it might have been left over from her earlier life, part of the nefarious stock-intrade of the harlot? If so why did she still have it? Is it quite the sort of vain luxury one would expect to find in the house of a devout Christian lady? Why had she not sold it and given the proceeds to the poor, which, to give credit where it is due, was a pretty sensible suggestion? Why, on her conversion, had she not thrown the beastly stuff away? Obviously because it was not beastly stuff. It was very precious stuff, like so many good and lovely creatures it had been misused, it had been defiled, but like Mary herself, it was not to be destroyed but redeemed, sanctified, given to God, used for his glory. So Mary gave it, physically, passionately, in an impetuous outburst of love, the whole three hundred pennyworth: there was not much moderation about Magdalene. She never suppressed her sensuous nature or her bodily instincts, she sanctified them, she was never repressed or frustrated or inhibited. She simply stopped loving the wrong things and began to love God.

Might I suggest, if only as an aside, that meditation on the episode of the ointment of spikenard provides a great deal of teaching about the technique of the daily Office. Mary gave it generously, as objective praise, she poured it on Christ, almost thrust it at him, without bothering too much about what it meant to herself, certainly without bothering about the bewilderment of the bystanders. So it is with the canticles, collects and psalms: generous, selfless praise.

At first sight this would make sense if only St. Mary Magdalene had been more like her sister (Luke 10 : 40), if her impetuous, physical qualities had been directed towards bustling works of charity. If, having anointed the Lord and kissed his feet, she had rushed off to nurse the sick, if after running out to Jesus at the death of her brother she had rushed back to get the supper, in a way that would be more in character, yet Magdalene is the archetype of the Christian *contemplative,* which is of much interest and importance.

There is an idea that the contemplative is a peculiar sort of supra-human species, a 'spiritual' being without appetites and passions, someone whose flesh has withered and whose blood has dried up. Some of the less reputable books about mysticism, or even reputable works misinterpreted, perpetuate the same idea, but we have already noticed how the contemplative, far from evading his responsibility and leaving the world, is in the front line of the battle for world redemption. And the true contemplative seeks *world* redemption, redemption of all created things, not some cloud-cuckoo land of 'pure spirit.' It is Magdalene, the first of the contemplative saints, who shows so decisively that the highest forms of Christian prayer demand, not permit but demand, complete, virile, full-blooded humanity. It takes the whole man, consonant with all creation, perfectly to adore God. Strictly speaking St. Mary Magdalene was not changed into a contemplative, she always was a contemplative, at least potentially : it is always a risky business to guess too hard at what God intends people to be.

St. Mary Magdalene remains courageously at the foot of the Cross until the end, then she remains to the fore in all the Resurrection stories. She weeps, frequently, but always the strong tears of penitence ; perhaps she is the prototype for the mystical gift of tears which held so strong a place in fourteenth century devotion. As might be expected it was St. John, the mystic, who first fully understood the Resurrection, who looked into the empty tomb, empty but for the linen clothes, and 'saw'—understood—and believed. His was the sort of experience from which the school of

St. Victor developed its mystical theology, the linen clothes and the napkin wrapped together in a place by itself were symbolic creatures, and St. John correctly read their meaning with the deep spiritual insight which is dependant upon sense experience.

Mary, however, was the first witness of the resurrected Christ. Again, obviously, because Mary was more competent than any one, even than St. John, to distinguish between a resurrected body and a phantom : *because* she was a contemplative she understood physical things.

And of course you cannot divorce Easter from Christmas. Magdalene, friend and comforter of our Blessed Lady, ever reminds us that Christianity began, not with a new philosophy, a new ethic or a new mystical system, but with the birth of a baby.

How did she develop these incomparable spiritual gifts? this contemplative wisdom, this discernment of truth, this knowledge and love for God? By one pre-eminent method : penitence. 'The diversity of the saints,' writes Archbishop Goodier, 'baffles analysis,' but when we look through the Kalendar we see that the Church has tried to make some sort of practical grouping: there are Martyrs, Doctors, Confessors, Virgins, Matrons and so on—until we come to July 22nd : St. Mary Magdalene, *Penitent*. We might expect sanctity to be won by holy virginity, heroic martyrdom or dedicated motherhood, but not entirely and completely by penitence for sin. Yet that is the secret of St. Mary Magdalene. She climbed the purple headed mountain and saw, understood, discerned knowledge, discovered the truth. She proved that penitence does all that. If some very tidy-minded liturgist is disturbed by the single exception on July 22nd, I think I should advise him to place Magdalene amongst the Doctors.

X

Easter Parade

LENT makes no sense without Easter, keeping Lent peni-
tentially is useless without keeping Eastertide joyfully. We
must try to be Christians fully, completely and all the year
round.

There used to be a nice little tradition in rural England,
which in its more remote and civilized areas probably continues unperverted, called the Easter Parade. The village
girls secretly made themselves new hats and dresses which
were worn for the first time as they walked to church on
Easter morning. I can almost hear the indignation from
certain quarters : going to church is a very serious matter,
especially on Easter Day, and this kind of flippant vanity
is quite out of place. I am not quite so green as to miss the
possibility that some of the young ladies might enter into
all this with not wholly unmixed motives, but I am still on
their side.

The one point I wish to make in this final meditation—
if that is not too pretentious a word for it—is that, in spite
of risks which human frailty always involves, the fundamental idea of the Easter Parade is sublimely theological.
And the point is this : when a lady goes to an important
function to meet an important person, such as a royal
garden party or the Lord Mayor's reception, she is very
careful about her appearance, and spends a good deal of
thought in choosing exactly the right clothes for the occasion. It is not vanity but good manners ; she is not trying
to impress any one with herself, but to be correct in de-
ference to her host.

But Easter Communion is more important than all the receptions and all the garden parties. There we are to pay honour, praise and adoration, not to some distinguished citizen but to the King of Kings. It seems to me that the same principles of courtesy should apply.

Of course it will be objected that Holy Communion is a 'spiritual' thing, and that our Lord is not concerned with fripperies like hats and frocks; but, personally, I am not so sure: 'like unto us in all things, sin except'? If God initiated the sacramental principle in creation, whereby spiritual things are expressed through matter, and if he made such dramatic use of it throughout the whole process of redemption, it seems odd that he should suddenly deny its validity now.

The really intriguing question arises: what, in every unique case, is the right dress for Easter Communion? My guess is that any devout lady who took the matter to the Sacred Humanity in meditation and colloquy would find the experience rewarding. She would not be concerned with an *ensemble* exactly right for the Mayor's reception that would also do well enough for Easter. She wants something exactly right for the Lord's Supper which therefore *must* be right for any other occasion whether the Mayor approves or not. She needs that which exactly and perfectly expresses herself, her real self, her 'spiritual' self, her baptized self, that which gives back to Christ the maximum of glory that he has given her. The village girls ought obviously, in all possible ways, to manifest the fact that they are Christ's adoring daughters.

It might even be helpful to defy the latest dictates from Paris and Bond Street and meditatively to follow the saints instead: Margery Kempe, the Lord's 'dearworthy darling,' wonderfully gay and flowery, the Swedish Bridget in plain black, Catherine of Siena in sensible grey, and perhaps a crinoline for the Little Flower? I am probably completely wrong with the details, but they would be completely right, or would our Lord prefer Easter congregations all in shapeless sackcloth? I cannot be dogmatic about the answer, but it is a good question. If the village girls first meditated seriously, and then made the frocks instead of some more frivolous amusement, it would not be a bad Lenten exercise.

I prefer not to bother with the masculine aspect, except perhaps to guess at just two answers from the Sacred Humanity : a kindly Chestertonian chuckle at a frock coat, and a rather louder laugh at a clerical collar.

But let us remember that golden rule that Satan forgot, and not take ourselves too seriously. All I am really trying to say, if Mrs. Alexander and George Herbert will permit some italic emphasis, is this :

> *All* things bright and beautiful,
>   *All* creatures great and small,
> *All* things wise and wonderful,
>   The *Lord God made them all.*

> Let *all* the world, in *every corner* sing
>   My God and King.